THE ONLY

ONE STOPPING

YOU, IS YOU!

How to Redefine

Your Limits

&

Redesign Your Life

MATT MATTHEWS

The Only One Stopping You, is You!

MATT MATTHEWS

First published 21/12/2012 By Matt Matthews, Copyright ©.

Matt Matthews Enterprises
www.mattmatthews.co
admin@mattmatthews.co
+44 (0)203 292 1391

This publication employs archival-quality paper.

A CIP record of this publication is available from the British Library.

Paperback edition, ISBN: 978-1-908552-18-1
Hardback edition, ISBN: 978-1-908552-36-5

This book is dedicated to anyone and everyone that sincerely wants to make a positive difference within their life and become the best that they can be, in order that they can then contribute in some way toward the betterment of humanity.

"Your playing small does not serve the world. There's nothing enlightened about shrinking so that other people won't feel insecure around you. As we let our own light shine, we unconsciously give other people permission to do the same. And as we are liberated from our own fear, our presence automatically liberates others."

— Nelson Mandela

"There are two primary choices in life: we accept conditions as they are, or we accept the responsibility of changing them."

– Dr. Dennis Waitley

"Everybody has genius, but if you judge a fish by its ability to climb a tree, it will live its whole life believing that it's stupid."

– Albert Einstein

TABLE OF CONTENTS

ACKNOWLEDGEMENTS

I sincerely express my unwavering love, trust, gratitude and respect for the Supreme Creative Intelligence of the Universe, without which, none of this would exist.

FOREWORD

Matt Matthews (born Matthew Hunt) is a London based Self Help Author, Inspirational Speaker and Peak Performance Strategist.

Born and raised on a council estate in Southwest London until his mid teens, throughout his adolescent years Matt was no stranger to varying degrees of poverty, violence, marginalisation, expulsion from school and even incarceration.

Although, these are all things unworthy of glorification, mentioning them serves only to provide the contrast between where Matt once was, and how he has been able to triumph through countless adversities to become the successful self help author, and inspirational speaker that he is today.

Although he had already begun upon his quest to *improving* himself, Matt was introduced to his first self-help book at the age of nineteen. And this is where he began to *reinvent* himself.

Having had enough of being a *"victim of circumstance"* he decided to instead become a *"victor of opportunity."*

Twelve years later, Matt has co-authored with some of the leading names within the field of personal development. He has also empowered many people through his "Advanced Communication Skills training programmes" (ACSTPs), along with his instrumental role within a number of community based initiatives for overcoming adversity and raising self esteem.

Matt's own transformation from an echelon of low self worth, frustration and limitation, into what he has accomplished today, is, in itself, a testament to the power of the human spirit.

It's also a testament to the effectiveness of personal development when diligently applied. Matt has been able to *redefine his limits and redesign his life,* and he now takes great pride in helping others do the same.

It is this degree of firsthand experience and practical application, along with his sincere passion to make a difference which qualifies Matt, to present this book to you today.

However, you need not be from the inner city streets of London, in order for you to benefit from this book. The principles, techniques and insights are universal.

"The Only One Stopping You, is You!" provides keen insights that can be used by anyone wanting to break free from limitations and utilise their potential to a much fuller degree, amidst adversity, or otherwise.

In closing: All of us have a great deal of unexplored potential just waiting to come alive. Likewise, all of us face some level of adversity throughout life.

Nonetheless, it's not just the type of adversity that we face, but more so, how we deal with it, that ultimately determines who we become.

Put simply: *This book is a must read for anyone wanting to express their excellence and utilise more potential!*

Johnny Wimbrey: International Speaker, Bestselling Author & Television Personality.

HOW TO USE THIS BOOK

For those already familiar with personal development, this book may simply serve as a refresher. For those new to the field it may serve as an eye opener. But whether familiar or new, those seeking a realistic and practical approach to self development will find it here.

Instead of vaguely scratching the surface, this book aims to offer a somewhat detailed overview on a range of concepts within the field of personal development. However, by no means do I claim that my knowledge within this field is *absolute* and *final*, nor do I claim to be an expert. I am simply inspired to share my perspective at this point in time.

With that said, here are seven points to bear in mind as you read through:

1) Read with an open mind. Utilise what resonates with you most and put aside that which doesn't, until necessary. This information is not *the* viewpoint; but, *a* viewpoint.

2) Take your time. Do not attempt to apply everything at once. Many of the *techniques* provided can facilitate change; but it would still be wise to first grasp some of the underlying *principles* that support them.

3) The results that you are producing within your life will not improve significantly by the act of reading alone; but more so, by the *application* of that which is read. And this means *actively* read as opposed to *passively* read. Bring the book to life within your mind by engaging in

your own personal dialogue; and more importantly, participate in some of the exercises as you read through.

4) While taking notes is also recommended, you may just simply want to have a highlighter pen: highlighting the relevant parts for easy reference at a later date. This will help if you ever wish to quickly refer back to the information that you found most beneficial.

5) For your convenience this book has been divided into four main sections: *Achieving More, Becoming More, Utilising More, and Perceiving More.* And these sections have been referred to throughout as *Cornerstones.* Each Cornerstone has been subdivided into chapters pertaining to its subject matter. This book can either be read from front to back or you can simply skip to a topic that interests you. Although they follow on from one another each chapter or Cornerstone can also be read individually.

6) *Cornerstone Four* explores information relative to human perception, the brain, and the mind as we know it. If you are unfamiliar with such concepts please do not let this deter you. This is one of the most valuable *Cornerstones* and may simply require a slightly more diligent level of study. This is true even though substantial effort has been made to simplify the concepts that are discussed therein.

7) Toward the back of this book you will also find a section entitled *Test Your Knowledge.* This is a quiz based solely on the subject matters found throughout. *Test your knowledge* provides an additional chance to fortify any

new findings in a challenging but fun manner by testing yourself on your favourite chapter or Cornerstone. This can also be applied as a beneficial addition if you wish to teach, and test, others on such topics.

In addition to the above points, if you are an adolescent this book can also be used as a guide for your transition into adulthood, as it may help you to avoid some of the snares that young adults experience while experimenting blindly.

Nonetheless, whether you are a young adult, an adult, or a senior citizen; with the utmost love, respect and integrity, I sincerely welcome and congratulate you upon your quest of self development.

I am humbled to share some of the valuable insights which have transformed my life for the better, and I do so with resolute faith that they may also do the same for you.

INTRODUCTION

Jim Rohn once said:

"Formal education will make you a living, but self-education will make you a fortune."

And although it is often used synonymously with money, the word *fortune* also translates as *destiny*.

What better way to shape your destiny than to unlock a greater degree of your dormant potential through self-education? It is no secret among the wise that: life is not solely about *having* more, but life is about *becoming* more, and we achieve this by way of active self development.

While it is true that *self development* can be dependent upon various aspects of knowledge, such as: cultural knowledge, spiritual knowledge, academic knowledge, and the knowledge of human characteristics and attributes (to name a few); this book is primarily focused on the latter. However, the significance of the other aspects above should not be overlooked, especially in today's modern world.

One of the key benefits of strengthening your knowledge of certain human characteristics and attributes is that you will then become more aware of how to identify and replace some of the *self imposed limitations,* which can often inhibit your potential.

Furthermore, it's possible that up to this point many of those limitations may have been subconscious, and therefore obscured from your immediate awareness.

Nonetheless, as a result of overcoming these limits you will be empowered to express a greater range of your infinite potential. And this is important because you can only utilise this power to the same degree that *you* are aware of its existence.

Naturally, you will then clearly see through the veil of societal conditioning which promotes the acceptance of material means (money, technology, etc.), as the *only* solution for our troubles.

Although they can and should of course be utilised; we must also acknowledge that we have access to much greater resources then these material means. Many of our most precious resources are those which are innately felt through the spirit, cultivated by the mind and expressed through the character.

Truth be told, we Human Beings are still a marvel unto ourselves. *Many of us* remain oblivious to the fact that *all of us* have untapped potential that can be brought forth, once we make the firm decision to do so.

However, we are now in a day and time where the sincere enquirer is sure to discover and utilise a greater degree of their potential power.

As a *being* that is connected to all that exists, it is beyond any reasonable doubt that you are capable of far greater things than you may even care to consider at this point in time. Nonetheless, it is *never* too late for any sentient being to unlock this dormant potential once they are *willing*.

I respectfully challenge you to acknowledge the fact that you, and only you, have the power to redefine *your* standards; *you* have the power to redefine your beliefs, and *you* have the power to *redefine your limits*.

We can only point the finger outside of ourselves for so long. In *escapism* there is always someone to blame; in *reality* we are the sole masters of our destiny.

We either allow the external influences of a manufactured society to completely govern our destiny, or we utilise our innate abilities to rise above them; and in so doing, regain our true power as a people.

We are all presented with innumerable choices throughout life, but once we are "in-the-know," those choices essentially become our very own responsibility.

You can *choose* to become the master of your thoughts, therefore the master of your emotional state, therefore the master of your *destiny*.

If at any point *you choose* not to do so, or even if you choose not to read on, then remember, in essence…

The Only One Stopping You, is You!

THE FIRST CORNERSTONE OF POTENTIAL

Achieving More

Chapter 1

THE PRESENT OF PRESENCE

"Many look to the past, yet many more look to the future; but the true essence is felt, within presence itself." – Matt Matthews

S top! Before you go any further, take a moment to consider this question: How many times throughout the day, do you find yourself reminiscing on the past or wondering about the future?

You are probably unable to answer this question with an accurate figure, but it could still be worth some thought.

When constantly thinking about what has *already* happened (past), or what *could* happen (future), we become less aware of what is actually *happening*. And as a result life passes us by.

Throughout this chapter we'll take a look at why it's important to embrace *presence*; and why when we approach new opportunities with views that are rigidly constrained by the past, it limits our self expression and therefore our potential.

This philosophy doesn't negate the importance of referencing the past for a cultural or historical sense of identity, but instead, it simply inspires us to gain more freedom from any misfortunate events that have occurred within *our own* lives.

Some of us may have experienced certain *traumatic* events in our lives and the aim of this chapter is not to make light of these. But with that said, it is still essential that we do not allow ourselves to become prisoners, trapped within the four walls of our own regrets, doubts, hostilities and fears.

The most common prison that people live in is the one built within their very own minds. This is where they stay *locked* into one way of thinking, behind the *walls* of self-doubt, and in *servitude* to their fears. While the intention of this book is to offer some of the keys for those locks, it is *you* that will need to put them to use and open the door to new possibilities.

You are the architect of your life and as such you are designing it daily. You are designing by way of the thoughts that you think, the decisions that you make, and the actions that you take; all of which you have the ability to control!

The power to *redefine your limits and redesign your life* belongs to *you*, and by keeping this idea in mind you will develop more drive to express your potential. Furthermore, you develop this *drive* because you become the *driver* of your life's journey. No longer are you merely the passenger.

As the *driver* you can see your past in the "rear-view," the future through the "windscreen," but you are still fully *present* to your control of the "steering wheel." *You determine your destination.* And you cannot focus properly on the road ahead if you are constantly looking in the rear-view mirror.

But on the other hand, if you are the *passenger* then you are merely just admiring the scenery. Worse still; you are helplessly at the mercy of an unpredictable driver, and that driver's name is, *life.*

The main difference between these two positions, driver and passenger, can be summed up with one word: *responsibility.* Once you develop the drive to express your potential and stay focused on your journey, then you are no longer just admiring the scenery. You have taken full responsibility for your "vehicle".

The Blame Game

With response-ability comes power. With excuses comes weakness. And one of the most typical ways that many of us avoid responsibility is by playing *the blame game.* That is; constantly finding someone, or something, else to blame when things don't go according to plan.

> "With response-ability comes power. With excuses comes weakness."
> #TOOSYY

But the more we keep pointing the finger at others is the more we are indirectly communicating to ourselves that we are not strong enough to override them. As a result, we continue to be the *victims*, rather than the *victors*, of circumstance. We also then fail to seek our salvation where it most typically resides: within ourselves.

To put it another way: when we habitually point the finger for any and everything; the very act of doing so momentarily renders us powerless to some external influence.

Anytime that we say something to the effect of: "They made me do it!" we are admitting that something or someone else has *full control* over how we feel and behave. Instead of thoughtfully responding, we (knee jerk) react. But whenever we are not response able, we are not responsible. Thus we remain at the mercy of external factors.

If we keep this idea in mind then we begin to gain greater self control because we stop mindlessly allowing external influences to determine our moods, thoughts, decisions and actions.

The next level on from this is that we also become more aware of our ability to attract the persons, places and things which are directly in line with our most dominant thoughts.

We realise that what we think about the most, determines what experiences we notice in the world. So if our thoughts are negative then we continue to manifest the corresponding experiences. But the same also applies vice versa with our positive thoughts. In this sense, we are shaping our own reality.

We are today where our *thoughts* have brought us, and where we'll be tomorrow is dependent upon our thoughts today: *in the present*.

Our ability to gain better control of this process is strengthened once we accept the responsibility of doing so. We are then less inclined to slip into the blame game. *We either accept conditions as they are, or we accept the responsibility of changing them.*

Yes Absolutely

Now let me ask you a quick question. Would you say that it's possible for you to express even greater potential than you already are? I'd say, *YES.* Absolutely! The real question is: *How much do you want to do so?*

If you want it enough ... and I mean *really* want it ... then you will be compelled by all means to do so. This is especially true if you're driven by the intense motive of a greater purpose. Put simply, we all have some reason why we want to succeed or do great things but; *is your reason bigger than you?*

When we feel as though we have a definite purpose to fulfil, we are not only highly motivated but we are highly inspired. We either find a way or make one, defeat is not an option. Some of us may already have an idea of what we believe to be our purpose, while others may not.

If you fall into the latter, do not lose encouragement. As the old English proverb states: *"Where there is a will, there is a way!"* Once you follow through on some of the exercises within this book you will gain additional clarity, along with a stronger sense of purpose. And this is true regardless of where you may have started out.

In fact, with the greatest of respect: no matter what you have been through, or whoever once told you that "you couldn't achieve this," or "you wouldn't amount to that;" *you still have the power within you right now* to excel far beyond those old opinions or circumstances. We all innately have the power to do great things. Do not forsake this power by continually rerunning negative memories on "instant-replay". Because the more you are there (in the past), the less you are present.

The same principle applies when we excessively focus on our *own* past errors, mistakes and so called failures. In fact, this is a very common cause of unhappiness. Some of us continually condemn ourselves by overly *focusing* on past errors, but doing so can sometimes only make us more likely to repeat them.

Focus on errors, and you will make more errors. Instead of continually focusing on the mistake itself, just simply acknowledge the lesson that you learnt from it, and move on.

Imagine a sportsperson going into a new game while continuously focusing on some past defeat. They'd be likely to lose again if their focus was on losing. Yes, they would have *learnt* from their past defeat but they wouldn't be overly focused on it. The same often applies on the playing field of life.

If you have had some relatively dismal experiences in the past, then don't allow yourself to be yet again defeated by your continuous need to keep looking back at those events.

Certain Experiences

In his book, *A New Earth* (3), Eckhart Tolle shares another fairly well known analogy, in Zen Buddhism, which similarly illustrates this principle:

Two Zen monks, Tanzan and Ekido, were walking along a country road. The road had become extremely muddy due to the torrential rains.

After walking a short while, as they neared a village, they noticed a young woman who was trying to cross the road. The challenge which this young woman had was that the mud was so deep on the road, that it would have totally ruined the bottom of her beautiful silk kimono.

Upon realising this, Tanzan immediately picked her up and carried her safely to the other side, her kimono unmarked by the soggy mud on the roadside.

The monks walked on in silence. Five hours later, as they approached the lodging temple, Ekido couldn't resist any longer. He exigently asked Tanzan. "Why did you carry that girl across the road? You know we monks don't do things like that." To which, Tanzan calmly replied, "Ekido, I put the girl down ages ago, are you *still* carrying her?"

Have you noticed the parallel here? For Ekido, it may have been five hours later, but in many other cases five hours turns into five weeks, into five months, into five years, and so on.

How many of us unnecessarily hold on to *certain* negative memories of the past: regrets, grievances or grudges? How many more of us are continually lugging around that big old heavy rucksack filled with *disempowering* stories of our past?

Paradoxically, we then wonder why we're moving so slow throughout life and with such depleted energy. Would it not make sense for us to put down the weight, lighten the load, pick up speed and gain some momentum?

Indeed, for many of us, the past will always define who we *think we are* to a certain extent and this is because we often derive our sense of identity from past events; i.e. "I went through *this* and it made me *that* person", etc.

But the key here is not to allow your past to *solely* define what you see as possible for your future. This is where many of us become stuck: we project the past into the future while simultaneously wondering why it keeps repeating itself.

While it is essential that we periodically reflect upon the past to evaluate *certain experiences*, it's usually best if this is done with a *positive attitude.* Instead of magnifying the negatives, develop the positives.

If we are overly focused on the negative aspects then we only keep ourselves trapped within the corresponding emotional states. (We will look at some practical ways to combat this pattern throughout this book.)

Do not allow yesterday to hold today hostage. To put it simply, do not over-reflect on the past to the point that you unconsciously *dwell* there.

Always do your best to keep a fresh outlook on any present opportunities. Utilise the *Present of Presence.* At this point you might be wondering what I mean by the term: Present of Presence?

The Time is Now

Consider this briefly: the past and the future cannot tangibly exist within the present moment. This is simply because the *past* has already gone and the *future* is yet to come.

Therefore, within the present moment ... as in, *Right Now* ... the past and the future can *only* be given life through memory and imagination.

Yes of course, *memory* and *imagination* can provide us with *identity* and *direction,* but if we are *constantly* focusing our attention toward the past or the future then, by default, we limit our range of awareness within the *present moment.*

So when I say that we must utilise the *Present of Presence,* this simply translates as utilising the *Gift of Now;* which, in essence, is *life* itself.

When we are more present, aware, or in-the-moment; we notice and utilise more opportunities. These are the same opportunities that would have passed us by had our attention been continually focused elsewhere: past or future. And by use of these two words I am not only referring to the distant past or future, but even just an hour ago, to an hour ahead.

You may be familiar with the common phrase "living in the past." Well; the same can also be true at the opposite end of the spectrum when we find ourselves, "living in the future".

By this I mean that we pay little attention to the *present* moment because we are constantly seeking happiness in some future event. But even when that future event manifests we fail to appreciate it because our attention is focused on yet another future event; on and on the cycle continues.

This causes us to overlook the present moment as we are constantly in a state of heightened anticipation; with the result being less due diligence, needless multitasking and of course, less presence.

Now take a moment to ask yourself where you've been spending the majority of your attention. Is it past, present or future?

Am I saying that we should never reflect upon the past nor imagine the future? No, I am not saying that! Of course we must utilise our great gifts of memory and imagination. The point here is simply to gain a more balanced level of awareness.

If you have been focusing 80 percent of your attention span toward the past or the future (leaving only 20 percent presence) then these figures should at least be periodically reversed. Not only will you then become more aware but as a result, more resourceful.

Positively reflect on the past, plan for the future, but not to the point that you completely disregard the present. When we are less aware and less present, a great number of opportunities simply float on by.

"Stop waiting for the perfect moment to arrive. It's a myth"

#TOOSYY

The only real time is *Now*. Stop waiting for the perfect moment to arrive. It's a myth and exists solely within your imagination. As such it will always be at some point other than *Now*. Instead, why not make the present moment the perfect moment? Start where you are, use what you have. Unwrap the Gift of Now.

Aside from this, something else to consider is the practice of regular meditation. I maintain that this is one of the most effective ways to strengthen our *overall* sense of presence.

However, regardless of whether you meditate or not; sometimes it can be good to just pause, in fact, just stop, and ask yourself: what am I thinking right now? But don't attempt to answer this question, just notice how your awareness heightens as you become more present.

Now take a minute to simply consider some of the things that *really* matter in life, i.e., your relationship with your children, family, love, self development etc., *but stay present*. Do not allow the mind to wander off into the past or the future and if it does then just gently guide it back to the present moment by focusing on your breathing.

Sometimes we can become so preoccupied with the "day to day grind" that we overlook the simple things in life: along with the things which are innately most important to us. Yet oftentimes, the joy and fulfilment that the soul craves exists within these simple moments that we overlook.

It is in these moments of *presence,* and in doing those "simple things," that the soul becomes most alive and we begin to feel fulfilled.

Throughout this book you will find many simple techniques that promote this, and in doing so you will strengthen your relationship with yourself and boost your self-image, but please, do not get too carried away with the information itself. Remember, sometimes it can be good to pause. In fact, just stop! And be present!

Without bringing the limitations of the past or the preoccupations of the future, into the present; we are essentially free and in-the-moment. We are void of any self imposed constraints. Anything is possible.

Billionaires – From Scratch

The libraries are packed with biographies of men and women who believed just that: anything is possible. Many of whom started out with little or nothing, even homeless and totally poor. Nonetheless, their unwillingness to be defeated eventually excelled them far beyond those conditions.

In one of her articles for *Forbes Magazine* in the year 2007 (1), Tatiana Serafin stated that, according to her research; "almost two-thirds of the world's 946 billionaires made their fortunes from scratch, relying on grit and determination, and not good genes."

"Out of these self-made billionaires," continues Serafin, "Fifty of them are even college or high school dropouts, including: Microsoft's Bill Gates, Russia's richest man - Roman Abramovich (who was an orphan), Steve Jobs and Ralph Lauren".

Furthermore, according to another article entitled *Rags to Riches Billionaires,* published by "Smart Money Daily (2)," it is no secret that, *Oprah Winfrey*, also overcame overwhelming odds and still persevered, finally becoming one of the richest women on the planet.

Allegedly, the world's wealthiest novelist, *J.K. Rowling* was also "claiming 'state benefits' before her book, Harry Potter, was published by Bloomsbury."

Amancio Ortega, came from humble beginnings starting his business with just twenty five dollars, making dressing gowns in his front room, and through his passion and determination to succeed he grew his "living room business" into the Zara Clothing Corporation; *Anna Mogokong*, founder of Community Investment Holdings in South Africa; *Invar Kamprad,* founder of IKEA; *Li Ka-Shing*, founder of Cheung Kong Industries, and the list goes on.

Eyes on the Prize

"Well those people were given different opportunities from me" you might say. Which may, or may not, be entirely true. However, the point being made here is that they *took* their opportunities without allowing their humble beginnings to hold them back.

They did not allow the hapless events of their *past* to stifle their *present* outlook on the *future*. Instead, they took better control of the *present moment* and created their future how they wanted it.

I am not suggesting that *achieving more* in life and utilising fuller potential should always be geared towards financial gains, or wanting to become a billionaire. I have simply drawn upon the success stories of these tycoons as keen, and common, illustrations of what is possible.

We could apply the same principle to any form of success— whether financial or not—and there are countless people who have.

Keep your eyes on the prize, that is to say, the gift: *the present.* Opportunities are plentiful. Do not allow yesterday to hold today hostage.

Efforts

Statistically speaking, few people might expect someone who'd been expelled from four schools, with no GCSEs or A-levels (and no College or University education) to write, self-edit and self-publish their own book to a reasonably high standard. And yet here it is. You are reading it!

If nothing else, let the book that you are holding in your hands right now represent possibility. Had I allowed myself to be defined by any of these factors above, this book might never have been written.

Despite Mum's best *efforts* throughout my adolescent years, like most, I was rebellious and hard headed. By the age of sixteen I'd already experienced countless run-ins with the law, incarceration, drugs, poverty, racism, violence, and even a brush with death. But I was not alone, others in my demographic also shared similar experiences.

A couple of years down the line I was then thankfully introduced to certain books which offered powerful insights into the possibilities of human potential. *"Lessons on unutilised human potential and the power of the mind; this is what they should've been teaching us in school,"* I remember thinking to myself.

It was around this time that I had one of my first major paradigm shifts:

I realised that the experiences of my past did not have to determine my vision of the future. And although I had a story to tell based on my past; I did not have to limit my potential because of that story. At any given moment, I was free to become whoever I wanted to be.

Regardless of where I was coming from, or how many times I'd been told that I was going to end up a "statistic," dead or in jail; regardless of how often, so many of us within my demographic were systematically marginalised and subconsciously made to feel inferior within society (undermining our self esteem). *Regardless of it all*; I could, *and I would*, *still* aim for the highest heights because, *my past did not have to determine my future.* And therefore, *anything was possible.*

Over a period of time, I was able to heighten my self-esteem and self-image. My life slowly began to transform from the usual outlook of frustration and indifference, to more productivity and purpose.

I share this with you, only to provide some insight on how I was able to turn my own life around by being committed to *self development*. Therefore, I do not present the subjects of this book to you based *solely* on "textbook knowledge," but instead, the firsthand experience of overcoming considerable adversity.

Nonetheless, this is by no means exclusive to me. If I can do it then *you can do it.* It all starts with a simple decision.

The fact that you have picked up this book today (and have read even this far) confirms that you too have made a decision. You have taken yet another step of the necessary action toward unleashing your greatness. You were guided here for a reason.

Remember, your past does not solely determine your destiny, the decisions that you are making in your life *right now* do. Every single day, we are literally shaping our tomorrow. I truly believe that as you read these words, you have a desire to fulfil your potential and find your true purpose.

I also believe that you *feel* as though you are worth so much more than your current circumstances might portray. In fact, in your heart, you *know* that you are worth so much more, and guess what? You absolutely *are,* so much more.

Well, now it's time to manifest more. Once you take the necessary *action* by applying even a few of the basic principles within this book, a shift will occur within your way of thinking. And this will naturally radiate to your way of being.

You have the power to change anything that you want within your life, and the best thing is that you can start that process right *NOW, by utilising the present of presence.*

So, *now* that we have a better understanding of *the present of presence,* and will thus utilise it to gain more freedom from disempowering memories of the past; what's the best way to plan for the future?

Well, one effective method is simply to set some goals that we can head toward. However, it's not solely about just setting the goals: goal setting is one thing, but it is just as important to become good at...

Chapter 2

GOAL SCORING

"If you don't have a vision for the future, then your future is threatened to be a repeat of the past." – A.R. Bernard

Imagine it with me: There I was, at one end of a football pitch standing by the goal with the ball at my feet. My coach had promised a reward if I could score a goal in the opposite end within two minutes.

There was nobody else on the pitch but me; all I had to do was dribble the ball to the other end and kick it in. Easy, right? Now, although I was alone on the field itself, a fair number of people stood at both sidelines throughout the entire length of it, just watching.

I began dribbling the ball down the pitch. That's when one of the spectators rudely shouted out, "It's not possible; you should quit!" Another one said, "What's the point? It's not worth it!" And before long, a lot of them had joined in. I heard things like, "You won't get any reward even if you do score the goal!"; "I tried and failed, so will you!"; "Don't be silly, be realistic!" and many other discouraging remarks.

As I got about a quarter of the way down the pitch, I looked up and saw a close friend in the crowd. He had one of those "what's the point?" expressions on his face. Uncertain of how great the reward was going to be, I momentarily lost focus. I paused and went over to him to see if he knew what the reward was, and if there was really any point to this task.

Just as I was about to ask him, I felt something hit the back of my head. I immediately turned around and saw an apple core on the floor rolling away. It had been thrown by a spectator over at the opposite sideline. I began making my way across the field to challenge his foolish actions.

But just as I got there, yet another object came colliding into my back. I paused, turned around, and saw an eggshell down by my feet. Someone had thrown a raw egg which was now running down the back of my T-shirt. Looking over to the first sideline, I saw someone rudely laughing and pointing! Of course, I now began to head in that direction again.

But with all my back and forth from sideline to sideline, I was spending so much time focusing on the spectators that before I could accomplish anything, my two minutes were up—and I was still goalless. I never did find out what my reward would have been, and it was all due to my own lack of focus and determination.

Now, of course, the details of this story aren't really true! And this probably wouldn't happen to anyone *exactly* as I've described it here. But still, on a metaphoric level this type of story is happening to many of us, every day.

Think of it in this sense: the soccer pitch is our own "*playing field*," the apple cores and eggs are the *doubts and criticisms* of others, the goal is our *vision*, and of course; the spectators are *still* the spectators.

Much time and energy is wasted by running back and forth challenging spectators who are quick to throw their doubts and criticisms when we are aiming for our goals. Furthermore, sometimes it's the spectators that doubt and criticise our ideas the most that are *no more qualified* than we are within the given area.

Apple Cores & Eggs

Most of us have also experienced similar parallels to the foregoing metaphor at some point in our lives. We had barely begun upon the path toward a goal that we wanted to achieve and then along came the spectators on the sidelines of our pitch.

They began throwing their *apple cores and eggs* of doubts and criticism, giving us all the reasons why our plans couldn't, wouldn't or shouldn't work.

At the time, if our willpower was strong and we were determined enough, then perhaps we simply ignored their remarks and continued on with our plans; however, if our willpower was weak because we hadn't strengthened our resolve, we probably began to water their seed of doubt by thinking thoughts like, *"Well, they might have a point."*

On the other hand, perhaps we outwardly challenged them on their opinions, which only ended up with us becoming increasingly frustrated with their stance, and therefore engaging in unnecessary debates or arguments.

But had we only just ignored the noise from the "sidelines" and continued to focus on our goal with fierce determination, we could have utilised our time and energy to much greater effect.

While it is true that some of these spectators may have had (what they considered to be) a legitimate cause for their dissuasion, it's likely that others were not so genuine. And concerning the latter, it would always be wise not to take their opinions to heart.

In many cases, other people's opinions say more about them (and their way of thinking) than they do about us; remember this and you will become far less dependent upon them.

Unless *absolutely necessary,* it would also be wise to resist the temptation of outwardly challenging the spectators for ego's sake. Because when we engage in unnecessary debates and arguments, not only is it a great waste of our time and energy, but we only become further entangled within their web of negativity.

Therefore, firstly: if you are to begin *achieving more;* it is essential that you do not become easily sidetracked by the spectators when they're throwing their apple cores and eggs; even if they hurl them unexpectedly and catch you on the blind side; stay on the pitch, in the game, and away from the sidelines.

"Your ability to keep your poise and stay focused in the face of doubt, slander, criticism and adversity is the real measure of your character."

#TOOSYY

Your ability to keep your poise and stay focused in the face of doubt, slander, criticism and adversity is the real measure of your character. Will you fold, or will you "keep calm and carry on"? It's not what happens to you, but it's how you *respond* to what happens to you. This is what reveals the true strength of your temperament.

Secondly: it will also help to maintain your focus, *on goal,* if you have a vivid and effective strategy on how to score that goal before stepping onto the pitch. This will help to strengthen your concentration toward the task at hand; thereby blocking out the why's and wherefore's of those at the sidelines.

Goal Setting vs. Goal Scoring

A vivid and effective strategy towards goal setting can be a very important part of achieving notable success in any endeavour. It is however, just as important to become as good at what I call *goal scoring;* as it is, goal setting. *Goal scoring is the execution of an effective strategy which will lead to the attainment of the goal that has been set.*

Other than contributing to a sense of direction, merely setting goals alone will not promote success, but taking the necessary action toward the fulfilment of them will.

We all have certain types of goals that we would like to achieve ranging from the mundane to the substantial; but sometimes, with the majority of our attention absorbed within our day-to-day routines we fail to lift our gaze above the banal and set *vivid* long term goals.

Consequently we end up with short term aspirations which are
the product of a limited scope of vision: perhaps a vague plan
for a week or two ahead. Ask yourself, "Where do I plan to be in
five years?" If you cannot immediately answer this clearly and
concisely then the chances are that you have an impediment of
long-term aspiration.

"Well anything *could* happen in the next five years" you might
say; which is true, it could. But guess what? Anything *couldn't*
happen in the next five years too, so you might as well have
some sort of long term plan; you have nothing to lose either
way.

A major benefit of having vivid goals is that they help to keep us
focused with a sense of direction. This does not only apply to
the semi-immediate goals—ranging from a few days to a few
weeks ahead—but also the mid-to-long term goals, which are
just as essential.

One Simple Question

Once we have clearly defined our goal and our planned course
of action toward it, it becomes clearer what situations we should
preferably avoid.

Before we take part in some new scheme, or endeavour, we need
only ask ourselves one simple question: *If I take part in this, is it
going to advance me toward my goal?*

When necessary, asking ourselves this simple question can
prevent us from being needlessly distracted by the relatively

unimportant "sideline" events, while maintaining a focused and progressive course of action toward our goals.

Focused concentration and willpower are the forerunners of mastery.

#TOOSYY

Sometimes the things that we fuss over today bear little relevance tomorrow, and in a week or so they are completely forgotten. The energy and attention dispersed on these matters could be utilised to greater effect focused "on goal."

No person can utilise their full power while needlessly dispersing their energy in multiple directions. Concentrate your forces. If you are serious about scoring your goal then harness your energies and direct them fully to that end. Focused concentration and willpower are often the forerunners of mastery. Do not become a "jack of all trades but a master of none."

It is often said that one must beware of wolves in sheep's clothing; well, similarly, it is also wise to beware of distraction, in opportunity's clothing. Determination is a one way street, stay focused on where you're heading. Sometimes what looks like a shortcut is actually a dead end.

Peter Drucker once said *"The best way to predict the future is to create it."* And this is certainly true. But while doing so it would also be wise to give a little due deliberation to the possible obstacles that may arise along the path.

Simple Signs

If there are any particular issues that you feel could prevent you from *goal scoring*; then here is a quick, simple and effective brainstorming technique inspired from the work of Robert Greene and Curtis Jackson within their book: *The 50th Law* (4).

First, write down the proposed issues. Next, draw an arrow from each issue toward your future goal. Now write down the answers to the following questions:

    I)   Does this issue prevent me from scoring my goal, or is it a "sideline" issue?

    II)   Would this issue evolve into something unnecessary if it's not addressed now? If so how?

Now, *very briefly,* take a moment to reflect on a past situation where you made an error related to a similar issue.

Usually, when we look at certain situations in retrospect there are some signs as to how we could have avoided those situations. And those signs often seem so obvious afterwards.

Once you have specifically identified what those obvious signs *were,* look at your current circumstances and ask yourself: are there any similar signs that I am overlooking right now? And if you identify any, be specific about what they are and how you plan to overcome them.

These are some of the finer points that many people tend to overlook when setting their goals, hence they rush out blindly, fail, and then think that it's because they're unworthy. It was just a little more due diligence that was needed.

Goal Specific

Before taking action and *goal scoring,* when setting goals our chances of success are greatly improved if we are vividly specific about what we want to achieve.

If we set goals that are too vague then, by default, we are allowing ourselves far too much room to manoeuvre with distractions, and excuses, along the way.

Set a specific goal with a specific deadline for its achievement. Increase your chances of success by limiting any feelings of indifference that can be encouraged by having too many options. Be specific! Narrow it down! If you want to make a lot of money this year be specific with how much exactly, and by what date.

For instance, instead of using "I want to make a lot of money this year" for a new year's resolution—which is far too vague; use something like, "I will make £100,000 (or whatever the desired amount) by December the 17th 2013." Next, specifically identify a possible means of how you plan to achieve this.

Furthermore, why must you make this amount? If your answer is "just to have money," then once again, this is not specific enough.

In many cases it's not the money per se that we want, but it's what the money can buy. Specify that reason. The more specific you are the more inspired you'll become within. You will then be confidently enthusiastic when it comes to developing an effective strategy for the accomplishment of your goal.

Correct Strategy

I once heard that "strategy is like the bridge between an idea and its realisation into the world." An effective strategy is essential for goal scoring.

A positive outlook is good for visualisation, morale, inner-drive and self worth, along with many other things mentioned throughout this book. However, having an effective strategy is often just as important.

Consider the earlier mentioned football metaphor; but instead, imagine a *skilled* footballer aiming to score the goal, this time with players of the opposition there to defend. It's highly unlikely that he/she would just think positively and run straight into the defenders of the opposite team.

In most cases, yes of course, he/she would have a positive mental attitude concerning their ability to get past the defenders; but nonetheless, *they would also have a strategy on how to do so.*

That strategy would probably include the use of skills, speed, etc., and they would also have a strategy for where to shoot the ball in order to beat the goalkeeper and score the goal.

Whether, or not, you are a skilled footballer is not the point; the point is that there's a clear parallel to be drawn here because an effective strategy is a key component for *goal scoring*. And as mentioned earlier, having a strategic plan in place before we get onto the "playing field" helps to keep us focused.

> ## "Strategy is the bridge between an idea and its realisation into the world."
>
> #TOOSYY

However, with that said, sometimes you may be forced onto the field before you have the time to formulate a strategy; in which case you may need to find your way, learning through trial and error. Nonetheless, each time you make a mistake, you know what *not* to do next time. You are positively *developing* a strategy.

You can also study others who have already been successful in the given field. Find out which strategies worked for them and which ones didn't; this way it's likely that you will save yourself considerable time, in comparison with the trial and error method.

If one hundred people have been successful in achieving a goal that you want to reach and they have done so by doing something in a certain way, then chances are that you can do the same. Why reinvent the wheel unnecessarily? Save time by using a proven strategy.

Cultivating Flexibility

As per the common saying, "*If at once you don't succeed then try, try, and try again,*" however, you don't always have to "try" in the same way. Developing flexibility in your approach can be extremely essential; because while you may have identified a specific goal that you want to reach, you may still need to make adjustments in your approach toward its accomplishment.

It has been said that, *"The definition of insanity is doing the exact same thing over and over again and expecting different results each time."* The point here is that, if you cannot achieve your goal one way then use another, and if that doesn't work the way you had planned then, still, another.

Change your approach as many times as necessary. Do not become too rigidly dependent upon the same pattern. If we stay overly conventional in our approach toward our goals, we limit our scope of creativity and become more likely to quit at the first or second *hurdle of adversity*; not because the hurdle was too high, but because the "running approach" and "jumping technique" needed slight modifications.

Realism

Set realistic goals; if for instance you are currently on an average income, then instead of, *"I want to be a billionaire by the end of the year,"* how about aiming for £100,000 first? Perhaps even £20,000 saved or, better still, invested.

Does this mean that a billion pounds is impossible? No of course not; but perhaps just not as likely, dependent on your level of determination, your *Why*, and your business model.

Setting unrealistic goals and then becoming disappointed when we don't reach them can be a precursor of low self esteem. And this is particularly the case if we then generalise our *perceived* failure, in one area, as being indicative of our overall failure as a person; which is simply not true.

It is also likely that this same disappointment could be used at a later date as an excuse not to set that goal again, even though our circumstances may have improved. On the contrary, we need not habitually set goals that are too easy either, as they fail to truly test us. Therefore we inhibit our true potential for growth and development.

Setting goals outside of our comfort zone is essential for growth; however keeping them achievable is just as essential for morale. Of course, this doesn't mean that we shouldn't dream big. It simply means; dream big "realistically."

Break it Down

If the goal you are aiming for is relatively big you can always break it down into sections. Think of the specific goal that you are aiming for and now break that goal down into three steps, each one leading to the next.

Once you have done that; then break each one of those steps down into three even smaller steps. Set specific deadlines for each one. Write them down and cross them off from the list as you go along. Approaching our goals in this manner will make them seem less mountainous, and more doable. In addition, by using this method we can become even more readily organised.

It also gives us a chance to notice our accomplishments and give ourselves a "pat on the back" at each completed step, and this can help to keep our level of enthusiasm and morale high. Before we know it our overall goal has been reached, and we barely broke a sweat.

Yet another benefit of *breaking it down* is that it can shift our perception. This is true because if we want to reach a goal but see it as something big, within our minds eye, it may become blown out of proportion.

If this continues over a period of time then it can also affect our level of motivation, and as a result we may even begin to doubt our ability to achieve that goal.

Following on from this *breaking it down* can also prevent us from, what I call, "short circuiting;" that is to say, losing interest and giving up on a project half way through. And this is because with every section of the goal that is successfully achieved, it spurs us on to the next section with enhanced confidence and enthusiasm.

Time Keeping

Good time keeping is essential for organisation, commitment, and thus goal scoring. If we cannot reach a simple destination on time, then why would we reach any of our goals on time, if at all?

When we constantly fail to keep the time that we say we are going to arrive at a certain place, we are effectively failing on a commitment.

If we say that we will be somewhere by 1pm but then for no good reason we turn up at 3pm, and proceed to justify our lateness with an excuse—no matter how small—then once again, we are failing on keeping a commitment and thus we are lacking a degree of integrity. This can also have a ripple effect into other areas of our lives.

The little things in life can make big differences. If we are to become more effective at goal scoring, we must first learn to "goal score" the simple things; and we can begin this by keeping good time. Organization and integrity are paramount.

If you have a tendency to procrastinate, it would also be a good idea for you to overcome the urge to press the snooze button on the alarm clock in the morning. On a basic level, you will then begin to eliminate the habit of *putting it off.*

The snooze button encourages procrastination; we roll over and hit the button in order to *put off* waking up and getting out of bed. If you must use the alarm to wake you up in the morning, when it goes off, immediately get out from beneath the covers and sit up straight. This can help to promote assertiveness, particularly in the mornings.

Although this is not a one-size-fits-all method (some of us may need to wake up slowly, dependent on our age, certain health issues, physical restrictions etc.) for those of us with no excuses, the point here is; keep good time and limit the need to hit the snooze button in the morning.

Together; these two simple elements will contribute to you overcoming procrastination, and goal scoring, in other areas.

Visualisation

Visualisation is probably one of the single most important factors for goal scoring. Your chances of success will be immeasurably enhanced if you picture yourself with your goal already achieved as often as possible.

At least once or twice a day, close your eyes—preferably with no distractions—and imagine *yourself,* with your goal already accomplished, but imagine it with vivid detail and full bright colour.

Allow yourself to really feel those feelings of accomplishment and happiness. As you are imagining this, become intensely associated with it: are there any sounds that are present? Are there any people present? What's the weather like? Are there any particular aromas in the background? How is the feeling in your body? Paint as vivid a picture in your mind's eye as possible.

Generally the more of the five senses that you employ while visualising your goal already achieved, is the more vivid and effective this technique will be, regardless of how simple it sounds.

If it is the accomplishment of a certain amount of money that you wish to achieve then hear the sound of the paper rustling as you count it. How does it feel in your hand? Or imagine typing in the password for your online banking and seeing the desired amount, already there.

Imagine it within the present tense, rather than at some distant point in the future. Imagining it at some distant point, keeps it at some distant point.

Your physiology is equally as important, oftentimes we think about things in line with how we feel and how we feel can be greatly influenced by our physiology, particularly our posture.

Sit how you would sit, walk confidently how you would walk, talk assertive how you would talk, get yourself fully associated with the state you have visualised (more on this later).

Four Questions

When we set a goal that we want to achieve; by asking ourselves the following four simple questions we can ensure maximum clarification. The four questions are:

1. What will happen if I get it?

2. What won't happen if I get it?

3. What will happen if I don't get it?

4. What won't happen if I don't get it?

These are not trick questions. They are designed to elicit maximum clarification as to why you should achieve your goal. If you already have a specific goal that you have set, go ahead and ask yourself those four questions right now and really take some time to answer them honestly.

Perhaps there may be some goals that you thought were important, that are not; or some that you thought were not, that are.

Compelling Reasons

If you have a goal that you want to achieve; why *must* you achieve your goal? What is your reason? Do you feel your *Why* in the pit of your stomach?

One of the things that will greatly propel you toward the achievement of any goal is a deep-rooted and emotionally compelling reason as to *why* you *must* achieve it. Is your *Why* merely for superficial gain, or does it have substantial meaning? Is your *Why* bigger then you?

Whatever your compelling reasons, write them down, specify them and they will give you immense strength in the face of adversity, if you ever feel like quitting.

When times get tough and scoring that goal seems like an uphill struggle, with these driving forces behind you, providing they are compelling enough, you will move mountains to see them through.

If you cannot think of any reasons that you would deem compelling enough, then simply ask yourself; what am I really passionate about and what is stopping me from having, doing or being that, right now?

By taking some of these simple steps, we are now becoming more aware of any opportunities within the present moment, but at the same time we have a direction in which we are heading; a goal that we are keenly focused on scoring.

However, as we know, large scale success may not happen overnight and scoring our goal may take sheer perseverance. This is why, as important as it is for us to utilise the *present of presence*, in order that we may become more effective at goal setting and *goal scoring*; it's just as important for us to be able to…

Chapter 3

STEADFAST

"Nearly every person who develops an idea works at it up to the point where it looks impossible, and then gets discouraged. That's not the place to become discouraged." – Thomas A. Edison

It is said that the Bamboo plant is one of the fastest growing plants known to man. Under the right conditions it has even been recorded to grow an astonishing forty seven inches in a single day, however, if you were to plant a root seed of bamboo in the ground you would see very little growth for the first three years.

In addition to this; that seed would only make it through those first three years providing it had been properly watered and nurtured throughout that time. After this seemingly stagnant three year period, it has been said that the Bamboo plant begins to grow so quickly that if you stood beside one you would actually see it growing before your own eyes.

"What effect does this have on *me* and *my* development?" you ask. The answer is simple. None! It has no direct consequence upon your personal development. It can however, serve as a discerning parallel toward our level of inner-drive and willingness to steadfast throughout a process. This is especially true if it's a process where we may initially have some boringly slow results.

If we are truly to begin *achieving more,* it may be worth remembering this simple truth: those who produce significant results in life are nearly always those who appreciate that mastering any skill requires a *process.*

At first there may be "slow growth," but should you steadfast throughout then just like the bamboo plant, you will bear the exotic fruits of your labour, in abundance.

The Root Seed

Every goal, every result and every desire starts with an idea. An idea is the "root seed" of any, and every, form of accomplishment.

We all have moments where we experience brilliant ideas; and many of these are ideas that—if acted upon with resoluteness— could dramatically increase the quality of our lives. Yet *sometimes* we lack the motivation and perseverance to see them through.

And in the fast paced society of today, with so much at our fingertips, many of us have become accustomed to instant gratification; so even if we do get the motivation to start a new endeavour, we expect to see immediate rewards or we quickly lose interest. In addition to this, we can become so busy anticipating the big results that we habitually overlook many of the small results happening within our lives each and every day.

And this is where many of us fail to notice our progress and lose enthusiasm for our goals.

But remember, although you may not have the "big result" straight away, whilst in the beginning stages of your endeavour *slow growth is better than no growth*. And your ability to stand firm throughout a process, shrugging off any petty challenges as they arise, will unquestionably ensure your rewards.

Does this mean that you should keep "banging your head against a brick wall" if something is *clearly* not working for you? No, of course not! It simply means that you do not use any old excuse that you can somewhat justify, as a reason not to exert the extra effort for what you want out of life. A keen level of *steadfastness*, matched with *progressive action* is essential for goal scoring.

A Penny or a Million £££s

To further illustrate this principle of "slow growth," consider the *penny or a million pounds* question:

Would you rather have a million pounds transferred into your bank account right now, or would you rather start with one penny and have the amount doubled in size, everyday, over the next thirty days?

Sometimes, the simple things that are done with consistency are taken for granted. Nonetheless, over a period of time they can "add up," amounting to huge results. Let's take a quick look at what would happen if you chose the latter option of one penny doubled in size over the course of 30 days:

Day 1: £0.01
Day 2: £0.02
Day 3: £0.04
Day 4: £0.08
Day 5: £0.16
Day 6: £0.32
Day 7: £0.64
Day 8: £1.28
Day 9: £2.56
Day 10:£5.12
Day 11: £10.24
Day 12: £20.48
Day 13: £40.96
Day 14: £81.92
Day 15: £163.84
Day 16: £327.68
Day 17: £655.36
Day 18: £1,310.72
Day 19: £2,621.44
Day 20: £5,242.88
Day 21: £10,485.76
Day 22: £20,971.52
Day 23: £41,943.04
Day 24: £83,386.08
Day 25: £167,772.16
Day 26: £335,544.32
Day 27: £671,088.64
Day 28: £1,342,177.28
Day 29: £2,684,354.56
Day 30: £5,368,709.12

This could be an analogy to remember the next time that we feel discouraged because we haven't had that *instant* "big result" in some area of our lives. If it is the *real* results that we are after then 99.9 percent of the time, it will take exactly that: *time.*

Good Genes or Lucky Breaks?

Think of someone that you would class as majorly successful. This could either be in historical or present context. Take a moment to think of their great accomplishments, contributions and so on. Isn't this how we usually look at such individuals; from the angle of their fame?

Rarely do we consider the laborious process they endured in order to *become* who they later became. More than often we choose only to acknowledge their success while completely disregarding the failures and struggles they encountered and endured along the way.

From this perspective, it's easy for us to class the reasons for their achievements as "good genes" or "lucky breaks;" we might even think that they were blessed with a superior level of intellect or some other rare advantages. But if truth be told, oftentimes, it was more to do with their sheer steadfastness than any of the above.

Those individuals simply refused to live "run-of-the-mill" lives. They held themselves to a higher standard and, with resoluteness, were fully committed to manifesting their dreams into reality. As consequence they achieved the corresponding results.

These individuals—just like the Bamboo shoots—may have also had some boringly slow and questionable results at the beginning. But then sure enough, due to their ability to steadfast, they reached the point where their success rate began to "shoot" through the roof.

They applied the rigorous level of practice and perseverance required to master any art, and they did this in order to reach the levels of success that most of us know them for. With this as a viewpoint, it's fairly logical to conclude that we can all reach our desired levels of success.

First and foremost we need only accept the previously mentioned fact that mastering an art—whether that be an internal or an external one, *is a process*. And that process more than often will take fierce commitment *multiplied* by long term vision, and *divided* with the correct strategy. This way we end up with manageable goals, each one leading to the bigger picture.

If we keep this fact in mind upfront once we start a new process, we will be less likely to short-circuit and give up after a week or two of not seeing any major results. James Allen summed this up best in his profoundly concise book, *As a Man Thinketh,* when he wrote; "*In all human affairs there are efforts, and there are results. The strength of the effort is the measure of the result.*"

Remember; your level of persistence is usually directly in line with your level of belief in your ability to succeed. If you absolutely believe (as you should do) that you can achieve anything that you put your mind to, then nothing will stop you.

Inner Drive:

Being very closely linked to one another, inner-drive and steadfastness usually go hand in hand. We could look at the ability of being steadfast as: holding our ground, commitment, endurance, "backbone" and so forth (which as we have just covered, are all essential traits to possess). While on the other hand, inner-drive would be that vigour to keep pushing forward, gaining momentum and advancing toward the target.

A keen level of inner-drive is therefore highly necessary for momentum; without it we could become so steadfast or resolute that we stay in a somewhat motionless "hold our ground" type perspective, but without actually pushing forward and stretching our boundaries.

This motionless perspective could be seen as a type of border-line comfort zone where we stay committed to playing our cards excessively safe. In such a mindset, we run the risk of forsaking the great power to be gained from forward motion and thus momentum: inner-drive.

It is this inner-drive which compels us forward toward a predetermined target. And although there can be various contributing factors; this particular quality is largely catalysed by two primary qualities which are *passion* and *ambition*.

The passion is our *fuel* and the ambition is our *map* for the direction in which we are headed. It could be said that if any of these two catalysts are significantly deficient then our level of inner-drive will reflect this, resulting in a kind of motivational languish.

When our inner-drive is low, procrastination is born. We then become less decisive with taking action and our tendency to procrastinate becomes stronger every time that we entertain it. It therefore just becomes easier, almost habitual, to put things off. After a while, this cycle can also create background feelings of inadequacy, as we lose momentum and even faith in our own abilities to successfully achieve our desired outcomes.

> ## "Our tendency to procrastinate becomes stronger every time that we entertain it."
> #TOOSYY

Following on from this, ambiguity and indifference toward what we want out of life will inevitably produce the corresponding results. These are two factors seldom friendly with a dynamic inner-drive, or any notable success in life. By contrast they are more eagerly acquainted with mediocrity and excuse making, both of which produce run-of-the-mill results, if any at all.

Inner Drive & Language

Our level of inner-drive can also be frequently undermined even by the language we use on a daily basis. In essence, language is interpretation.

This is not only true of verbal language, but also imagery, symbolism, body language and so forth. Furthermore, one could argue that our entire conscious realities are based on—and constructed with—various forms of linguistics (interpretations of things), as this is how we decipher the world around us.

For instance, if we can't think of a word to describe something, how do we then comprehend and identify the existence of that thing by definition? We don't! With this in mind, it's hardly farfetched to concur that language itself has tremendous power in terms of influencing our feelings. And it can either greatly enhance, or undermine, our level of inner-drive.

Any efforts toward eliciting a positive state and building a dynamic inner-drive could be subtly undermined by our common and almost unconscious day-to-day use of certain words.

These are words such as: "*try*" which (dependent on the context) implies the possibility of failure from the onset; the word "*should*" which carries the associated feelings of burden, guilt and pressure; and even "*hope*" (again, dependent on the context) which omits responsibility and personal power by relying completely on some outside source for results.

There are many more of these words to consider (see: *using empowering language,* page 301). And as tempting as it may be to deviate into a full scale explanation of them right here, for now let's continue to explore some other factors related to this invaluable trait: inner-drive.

The Inner Drive of a...

There is a group of wonderful human beings that usually have an extremely high level of inner-drive; that's right, you probably guessed it: children. We were all children once right? Just think: usually when a young child wants something enough, they are very seldom easily deterred. Most children innately have a strong inner-drive when it comes to getting what they want.

In addition to this, if and when you ever ask a child; *"what do you want to be when you grow up?"* In most cases the child will usually reply somewhat assertively; *"I'm going to be a doctor,"* or, *"I'm going to be a scientist,"* etc.

I personally have never heard a child reply, *"I'm going to 'try' and be doctor"*, or, *"I'll see how it goes and if I can, maybe I'll be a scientist."*

Typically, most children dream big and with certainty, they are usually positively affirmative with their reply: *"I'm going to be a..."*

Does this mean that there has never been, or will never be, a child that replies with the *"tries"* and *"maybes"*? No, it doesn't mean that. But it's just more of an unlikely response from a young child because at that stage they are generally more optimistic and less likely to be rigidly accustomed to many of these doubt laden language patterns. In addition, they have far less a number of vicissitudes to relate those language patterns to.

Although many of us tend to succumb to various *seemingly* de-motivating experiences as we mature; this need not become a visceral fixture of attitude. By identifying and replacing the self imposed limitations (limiting beliefs) which are causing these de-motivating factors to occur as such, you can then reposition your stance towards them (more on this later).

Another example of the inner-drive that we posses during early childhood is our level of determination when learning to walk.

Most babies will undoubtedly fall on a number of occasions when learning to walk stably. In fact, it has been statistically stated by various studies that on average, babies fall down approximately three hundred times before eventually learning to walk stably.

Assuming that on average this number is correct; then this in itself is a prime display of the inner-drive and steadfastness that we all utilise as children. Can you imagine if, as babies, we tried out that *"walking stuff"* and gave up after failing at our first few attempts? How great was our reward of having the inner-drive to succeed in that area?

As you are reading this right now, no matter how prone to procrastination, resignation, cynicism or complacency you may have become over the years; were you aware that as a child you fell down, *and more importantly got back up*, approximately three hundred times before you walked stably?

If you were so naturally driven to succeed then, can you reinvigorate this inner-drive and do the same now? Of course you can! Act on this belief and you will naturally then become more productive, boosting your self-worth in the process.

Inner Drive & Self Worth

Inner-drive is also related to self-worth because as we are continuously taking action toward our goals, we cultivate and reinforce the belief that we can unequivocally achieve anything that we put our minds to.

Thus it becomes even more apparent that our greatest hindrances are our very own doubts and limiting beliefs; which ultimately determine what we consider as possible, or not. However, on a fundamental level, *all possibilities exist at all times.*

Start now! Take action to overcome doubt and inertia. Write that business plan, make that phone call, send that email or that letter, visit that person, work on bettering yourself, watch or listen to some personal development DVDs or CDs, read more of those uplifting and educational books—as you are doing right now, attend those seminars and mingle with positively progressive people. *Don't wait for a change of environment until you act: get a change of environment by action.*

Begin to doubt your doubts and push through those unnecessary self imposed limitations. It's time to commit to utilising a greater degree of your immense potential.

Taking all of this into consideration there is, however, one key attribute that makes it much easier for us to maintain our level of *steadfastness* and *inner-drive* while we are *presently* taking action toward *scoring our goals.* It is a quality that can significantly increase our energy levels in the face of adversity, and that quality is...

Chapter 4

PASSION

"There is no passion to be found playing small - in settling for a life that is less than the one you are capable of living." – Nelson Mandela

Early one summer Saturday evening, at the age of 14; I remember being on a high speed train with my friend at the time, Mark. It was a *fast train* from Surbiton to Clapham Junction and therefore didn't stop at the many stations in between.

Five minutes into the journey we got a phone call; one of our friends needed our help. We now had to get off this train at Wimbledon which was one of those stations that it wasn't stopping at. But being the unruly teenagers that we were that didn't bother us. We knew that if we timed it right, we could pull the lever for the emergency alarm and the train would automatically *have* to stop. Furthermore, we knew just how to time it and where to pull the lever (when we saw the tall white building on our left hand side), for the train to start slowing down and come to a stop at the platform of Wimbledon station.

Looking out the window of the speeding train, I saw the tall white building coming up, *fast* approaching. I pulled the emergency lever but the train was going so fast that my timing was slightly off. The train's automatic braking system went into effect as it began to slow down rapidly.

We could now see Wimbledon station coming into view but it was coming into view too fast. I hadn't timed it right, the lever had been pulled too late and the train would not stop at the platform how we had planned. Still rapidly slowing down, but going too fast to stop at the platform, the train went straight through Wimbledon Station and eventually came to a standstill about 150 metres up the track.

Determined to see this through, we opened the train doors and jumped down on to train tracks to run back to the platform. Mark went first and I quickly followed, but to reach the platform we had to cross over another two train lines.

Mark was so fast that he'd already crossed both train lines and was running along the gravel back toward the platform. But then just as I crossed the first train line, I heard a loud horn sound, "Woooh! Wooooh!" I looked up to my left and saw a *high speed* train coming toward me, and *fast*. It was easily doing over 100 miles per hour, coming at me head on, and no more than 50 metres away.

You've probably heard the saying: "*My life flashed before my eyes*" right? Well, *my* life flashed before my eyes. It was a defining moment, one where I would either freeze up from the shock or run for my life. Thankfully it was the latter. I quickly ran across that train line and jumped out of the way, onto the next train line, heading toward the platform. But it was then that I heard another loud horn sound, this time from my right side.

Again I looked up; *another* high speed train was approaching me from the opposite direction. I had cheated death once only to be faced with it again two seconds later. As this second high speed train approached me head on, yet again I saw my life flash before my eyes.

Time seemed to slow down as I saw the faces of loved ones rapidly flickering through my mind. It was like I had at least fifty images run through my mind at lightning speed as I momentarily looked at the train like a deer caught in the headlights.

Out of these flash images, oddly enough, the last one that I remember was of me MCing on stage in front of a large crowd. (At the time I was an aspiring MC in the Jungle music scene, but to make it onto the big stage—with other renowned MCs like Skibadee, etc., —was my dream, my goal, *my passion.*) That last split second image snapped me back to reality. It was almost as though I thought to myself, in a nano-second; *it's not my time to go yet, I haven't fulfilled my dream.*

I jumped out of the way; literally for my life. I felt the G-force hit me from the speed of the train as it once again sounded its loud horn and sped by. I had cheated death twice in no more than 10 seconds. I was extremely lucky; "stupid," but lucky.

Later on that night as I kept mentally replaying the scenario, for some unknown reason the most prominent part of the memory was that last thought that came to mind before I jumped out of the way of the second train: the thought of me MCing on a stage. It seemed as though that single (split second) thought of me *fulfilling my passion* had snapped me out of shock and literally saved my life.

Wild Fire

When we are passionate about something, we have a definite motivating force. We take action. Even in the face of harsh adversity we can triumph against seemingly overwhelming odds. The word *passion* itself can simply be defined as: something that we feel strongly about; or, *"a strong and compelling emotional state."* However, for this reason, it can also be likened to that popular chemical reaction known as Fire.

Kept within its limits, most of us would agree that fire plays a fundamental role toward our survival; and this goes from the sun, right down to the cooker. However, as necessary and beneficial as fire is, by contrast we need not go into any lengthy explanation of how dangerous and detrimental it can become, if not kept within reasonable limits.

A similar view could be adopted toward describing passion which, in essence, is emotion. And any "strong and compelling emotional state" can become wayward when left unsupervised by our rationality. Just as the uncontrolled *wild fire* can be dangerous; the same could be said of an uncontrolled *wild passion*.

Nonetheless; generally speaking, passion can be a key factor for achieving success in any endeavour because it is one of the most powerful driving forces known to man. Once this great driving force is channelled correctly, *guided by reason*, it translates into a keen enthusiasm to *achieve more* out of life. And in this capacity it has been responsible for a great deal of human exploration, persistence and triumph in a large number of areas.

An emotional driving force is considerably more compelling than a logical one. And with this in mind it's not difficult to comprehend that when we have a goal which is backed with a compelling emotional reason (passion) for why we must achieve it; our chances of doing so are increased, immeasurably. Success is almost certain before we have even started. To put it simply, we become much more determined: *We either find a way, or make one.*

When used productively, passion is one of the key factors that separates perseverance from quitting, excellence from mediocrity, a great piece of work from a good piece of work, high income earners from average income earners; and it is also the difference between, *will do* and might do.

Key Component

Developing a passion to succeed creates a sense of urgency, which dims the lights on indifference and complacency. With a healthy degree of passion set toward accomplishing something we become more resourceful. We begin to see the opportunity in every setback and the stepping stone in every hurdle, defeat is not an option.

If we were to illustrate a weak passion to succeed, it could be envisioned as a weak candle-flame; because although the lit candle may temporarily provide a glimmer of light in the darkness, it would still be easily *blown out* once we *"got wind of"* a setback. Does this mean that it's impossible to achieve a goal that we are not passionate about? No, it doesn't mean that. It merely means that we may need twice the amount of discipline to stay committed to those endeavours in the face of adversity, as they are most likely to produce a sense of burden and boredom rather than fulfilment and purpose.

Passion in a particular area makes it easier for us to sacrifice other superficial wants, and maintain a progressive course of action without being easily distracted. The good news here is that anyone can develop a passion for near enough any goal that they have. And, as we touched upon earlier, this can be done by being totally identified with a few convincing reasons for its accomplishment.

When we have a keen passion for a particular goal we can endure almost anything; but without it, many of us quit at the first hurdle. It can be increasingly challenging to successfully push through stern adversity if one is not passionate about the desired outcome.

Remember, this is not an absolutely uncontrolled *wild passion* which totally overrides all sense of reason, but simply the keen enthusiasm to *achieve more* out of life. In general, *follow your heart, but take your brain with you.*

Those of us who become successful in certain areas are nearly always those of us who are motivated to handle both the nobler, and the pettier, aspects of our mission. This is made easier when one *feels strongly* about the outcome. Overall, I maintain the viewpoint that, for our lives to have a strong sense of meaning and fulfilment we must have something that we are passionate about: something that easily motivates us, which we feel in our heart; the expression of a natural talent, a cause, a purpose, a mission.

However, by suggesting that we pursue things in line with our passion, this is not the case if that passion is fuelling certain types of self-destructive behaviours. These could include the infatuation with things like: alcohol, narcotics, overeating, junk-dieting, over-fornicating, cheating, compulsive lying, stealing, self-bodily-harm, and so on.

While it is true that many of these might appear to bring about some type of short-term relief, over time they only make matters worse. The pursuit of these negative desires is usually the result of a *misguided* passion, which is typically characteristic of an individual who is oblivious to their true scope of potential.

This individual may be unaware of a more positive and uplifting outlet that can be utilised in replacement of their negative addictions or behaviour. But once their energies are keenly focused on something productive, and their positive self-image is restored; great things are accomplished.

The following are a few simple insights and exercises that may help to identify, elicit, and cultivate a productive sense of passion.

Passion Board

The first thing needed here is a large blank poster board. Once you have your board, gather a collection of images of the things that you want to achieve. These could be commodities, or they could be certain positions that you aspire toward. You could even gather some of your favourite sayings, articles and any other inspirations in this regard. Stick all of these on your poster board, and now hang this board somewhere that you will have to look at it every single day, preferably first thing in the morning and last thing at night. The purpose of this is for you to keep a constant visual reminder of what you want to achieve.

Put simply; surround yourself with the images of your intention and direction. In doing so your awareness and passion toward such goals will grow, and as your board evolves you will keenly begin to distinguish between the activities that will keep you on path toward these goals, and the activities to be avoided which don't.

These things combined will instigate a set purpose, and once you are dedicated to realising this you will naturally move toward its accomplishment.

The Journey

We need not always attempt to reinvent the wheel through pride. To find out the tried and tested techniques, you could possibly study others who have already become successful doing what it is that you want to do. Figure out how and why they're able to remain successful, and then set up structures to emulate them until you find your feet.

Remember, it's not always solely about the end result. It's the process that you go through, and the *experience which you gain* along the way, that has the biggest impact upon your personal development. In this sense oftentimes the journey can be far more valuable than the destination.

Childhood Interests

If we are not too sure what we are passionate about, one way that we could possibly get an idea is to remember certain hobbies and interests that we had as children.

Of course, certain childhood interests may not be transferable into the adult world, so games like Kiss Chase or Stuck in the Mud won't count. But generally speaking, as we mature many of us tend to become increasingly disconnected from the things that brought us the most joy throughout childhood.

For example, some of us may be familiar with, Frank Lloyd Wright: considered as America's greatest architect. It is no secret that Wright played with wooden blocks throughout his entire childhood (5).

Are there any hobbies and interests which you were passionate about as a child that could be reinvigorated now? Would you feel fulfilled and purposeful within this area? Is there a market for such a service today? Could you potentially earn an income from providing this service or product? What would you need to do in order to achieve this?

Passion & Fear

When it comes to pursuing our passion, one of the greatest inhibitors can be the *fear of failure*. And this is commonly linked with the fear of what others might think of us. "Would I seem too unconventional or weird?" or "what if I fail, what about my reputation?" "People might think this, people might think that," so on and so forth.

This fear of failure is closely associated with the fear of rejection; both of which have their roots in our *need for belonging*, and our *need to be in control* of what others think or feel about us. But in actuality, *we* are the only ones that are in control because these fears are solely the by-products of our own imagination in the first place. In addition to this, only we have the power *to truly* decide how *we* think or feel, regardless of any external opinions or judgements.

Along with many others, these three fears: failure, rejection and loss of control—are ultimately the spawn of one central fear, *"What if I am not good enough?"* This central ego-based imaginary fear is the source of all comparatives. Does this make the ego bad? No it doesn't! The ego is an essential part of being human but like anything else, too much of it can be detrimental.

Becoming more aware of the ego, and then learning how to better utilise and control it, is essential for notable inward development. It is through the ego that many of us create our sense of identity, via our own mental concepts of where we fit in—within the world at large. And thus, it's our ego that is primarily concerned with comparatives such as, whether we are better or worse than others; when in reality *we are neither*.

Everything is fundamentally a part of the same source; we need only play our position, and we can do so by first identifying our life's true passion, and therefore purpose. With that said, of course there may be times where we are naturally inclined to compare ourselves to others, but if you catch yourself doing this needlessly then remember this: *"Don't compare. Prepare!"*

"Don't compare. Prepare!"

#TOOSYY

When this is truly understood the fear of failure—which in most cases is completely irrational—disappears. So does our need to make unnecessary egoic comparisons, conform to the status quo, or keep up with the Joneses. We then begin to substitute the *competitive* mindset with the *creative* one.

If you are particularly prone to imaginative worries of failure, the next time that you notice your mind leaning toward this direction, here is a more empowering angle to consider: *In life, there is no such thing as failure: only feedback.* This means that if a particular situation did not go as you had planned it; it has simply provided you with the valuable *feedback* of your actions, thus you learn how *not* to go about that task next time.

In fact, "failure" often produces amazing opportunities that sometimes go unnoticed. And the reason they go unnoticed is because we can become so tunnel-vision-focused on the door that closed, that we "fail" to see the two doors of opportunity either side of us that are wide open.

Personal Passion

Our passions are personal. They need not make sense to others as long as they are fulfilling to us. We would do well to remember that, the ideas of other people—about who we are, or who we should be—belong to *them*, not us. In the words of the great motivational speaker and trainer, Les Brown: *"Other people's opinions do not have to become your reality."*

Others are free to have their opinions of us, just as *we* are characteristically free to stand independent of their opinions. Although, essentially, we are all connected, we can still express our "uniqueness," as we all have some *sui generis* qualities to bring to the table: none of which are "better" or "worse," just different.

Awareness of Passion

Many people believe passion to be an attribute which, you either have, or you don't. Yes of course, some people are naturally more emotional than others but everyone has at least one thing they are passionate about.

Therefore, it's not a matter of having or not having passion, but more a matter of finding or not finding it, within ourselves.

Top Three

Yet another simple, and potentially passion-identifying, exercise is to list your top three movies. Once you have done this, think about the underlying theme of each. Do all three have a common theme in some way? For instance, when I was first taught this exercise I was asked the same question. My answer was that in the last ten years my top three movies would have to be, Inception, Avatar and The Matrix.

The common ground between the three is that they are all, increased-perception orientated, along with utilising latent powers of the mind to better effect; thus maximising once latent potential. It's no wonder that I have found so much passion in authoring this book which also explores exercises geared toward increasing our perception and, more so, *potential*. You could even do this quick exercise right now, if you haven't already.

If you're sincerely honest with yourself and your own personal choice of the top three, as opposed to that of your social circle, you'll probably be humbled by how closely the common theme throughout them hints at your passion.

Four Simple Passion Finders

1. If you had more time, you would love to...

2. Is there any activity that you do now, which you would still love to do, even if you already had everything you ever wanted?

3. If today was your last, what would be the number one thing that you would really regret not having done?

4. What would you say is the world's greatest need?

Your answer to any of these will hint at your passion(s). Next, we only need to take the necessary action in the appropriate direction.

OK. Now that we have discovered some techniques that will assist us with *achieving more;* how do we address some of the deeper self imposed limitations which form barriers along our path to *becoming more*? To find out, let's continue our journey into *The Second Cornerstone of Potential.*

The End of Part One

THE SECOND CORNERSTONE OF POTENTIAL

Becoming More

Chapter 5

SELF WORTH

"When you please others in hopes of being accepted, you lose your self-worth in the process." – Dave Pelzer

Life is not solely about having more, life is also about developing one's self internally and *becoming more*. By doing so we develop a stronger sense of self-worth; and the highest form of self-worth is generated by genuine self-love, which in turn is the result of self acceptance.

Love is to the soul like the heart is to the body; respectively without which, both turn cold. Love is the most powerful source of creativity and the human heart has the most powerful electromagnetic field within the body. It's no wonder that the two are so commonly referred to synonymously.

> "Love is to the soul, like the heart is to the body, without which both turn cold."
>
> #TOOSYY

Beyond any doubt, love is truly at the source of us *becoming more* mentally, spiritually, physically. With self-love we find self-worth. However, true self-worth is experienced not just from self-love, but more so the *genuine* love and contribution to all.

W.I.I-FM

Self-worth is a term that is typically used to represent someone's general assessment of themselves, and this can include any of the following: self-respect, self-regard, self-esteem, self-trust, genuine self-love.

Now, although the word "self" is the prefix of these five qualities, this is not to be confused with "selfishness" in the typical sense of the word. But in the broader sense of the word, a degree of selfishness can be required for us to focus on developing our own skills and attributes.

We can then guide others not just by rhetoric, but by example. Many people have good intentions but lack effectiveness because they have not taken the time to build themselves from the inside, out.

Furthermore, by way of active *self* development we are able to *contribute* more effectively and this is simply because we have more qualities to contribute. From this perspective it could be said that we must be "selfish" (focusing on *personal* development) in order that we may become more effectively "selfless" (contributing a greater scale of our attributes to others).

Once again, this selfishness is not to be confused with the typical sense of the word, whereby a person is so self-absorbed that they loathe contribution to others unless for their own personal gain.

This type of individual is only ever tuned into one frequency: W.I.I FM. (*what's in it for me?*) Disproportionately self centred, arrogant and self righteous, this mindset is often the result of poor self development, in the broader sense we just spoke of.

With self development we embrace the inward journey. We become more aware of our potential and our capabilities, thus developing a real sense of inner worth. We strengthen our integrity, embrace honesty, trust intuition, and emit love. We are then awoken to a deeper sense of self from which a heightened state of consciousness emerges.

We recognise the divine presence within us that is beyond the criticism, the opinions, or the judgements of others. As a result we too begin to criticise less, because we are less concerned with superiority. We realise that a superiority complex is often an inferiority complex disguised, and by default we become more aware of the common causes of low self-worth.

Common Causes of Low Self-worth

Low self-worth is a typical symptom of low self knowledge, triggering feelings of inferiority (in one of its many forms). Many of us are slightly deficient in this area for a number of reasons, some of which are the consequence of certain beliefs that we adopted throughout childhood: about ourselves and the world.

Low self-worth can also be the result of: constant criticism, lack of love, lack of appreciation, lack of expectation, *perceived* failure, *perceived* fear, low energy levels (often due to poor diet, lack of sleep or illness), procrastination, indifference, laziness, lack of variety, negative company, low morale, lack of purpose, and so on. All of which can lead to thoughts of inadequacy; diminishing our self-image in the process.

Ever ready to protect this fragile self image from some imaginary threat, we then sometimes become over defensive or hostile when faced with criticism. In fact, becoming easily offended at the slightest hint of criticism is characteristic of low self-worth; because when self-worth is low then the slightest affront can penetrate. To put it another way, we often become offended by criticism to the same degree that our self-worth is deficient.

Furthermore, those of us most sensitive to criticism are often those of us most critical of others. When we criticise and judge, we are more prone to thinking others are doing the same. But needlessly criticising others for inconsequential acts is a cheap way of validating our own sense of importance; and worse still, we do this with often false, needless comparisons. If kept up over time, this can lead to what I call unhealthy narcissism.

Unhealthy Narcissism

Unhealthy narcissism refers to when an individual is unnecessarily, and overly, pompous: continually looking down their nose at others, with a largely false aura of self-importance. This "front" is a self-protective mechanism designed to shield what is essentially a poor self image.

"An overt character trait usually disguises its opposite."

#TOOSYY

We've all heard the saying: *A dog that barks too often seldom bites!* And this is because an (unnecessarily) overt character trait usually disguises its opposite.

Unhealthy narcissism is an obvious sign of low self-worth because an individual is attempting to cover up a poor self image to the point that they habitually overcompensate. This is why I mentioned earlier that a superiority complex is often an inferiority complex, disguised.

Nonetheless, regardless of whether you have low self-worth or are unhealthily narcissistic, the truth is that you *still* have an abundance of unused potential and greatness within you. And it's just waiting to be called upon, *by you.* You are worth your weight in gold, *without the pretence.* Your character already has a *mountain* of value and purpose to offer the world, *without the pretence*; you simply need to acknowledge and embrace it.

If you have ever climbed a mountain you'll know that upon reaching the summit, naturally you admire the view around you: the different shapes and details of the other nearby mountains. In short, you admire the view *out there.* But you cannot truly see the beauty and detail of the mountain that you are already sitting on top of, and that's exactly why: because you are *on top* of it.

In this sense; that mountain you have climbed is your life, to date. It represents the "mountain" of experiences that you have assimilated, learnt from and overcome along the way. All of which have contributed to where you are at this moment.

Metaphorically speaking; if you have triumphantly climbed to the summit of Mount Tryfan then that is a worthy accomplishment; pretending that its Mount Everest is not. *Appreciate it for what it is.*

Accept yourself. Without self acceptance an identity crisis is inevitable. Embrace your "mountain." Play your part! Do not run from who you are by imitating the part of another. This is one of the quickest paths to depleted self-worth. How can we have self-worth if we do not even accept and know *self?*

Listen: there has never been a *You*, and there will never be another *You*. You are unique with specific gifts, talents, perspectives, attributes, to offer the world. Do not forsake this just to fit in. Stand out. Let your light shine. Be true!

Internal Greatness

Once we are true to ourselves we embrace the notion of self acceptance, thus we heighten our self-worth through genuine self love. With a healthy level of self-worth our lives gain a greater sense of meaning and we experience an inner fulfilment and a strong sense of purpose: we are *becoming more*.

All of us are here on Planet Earth for a reason, we all have an abundance of potential to be utilised; however, it's our awareness of this which is the key to its realisation. And this awareness can be increased by identifying our natural strengths.

A simple way to start building self worth is to identify your natural character strengths and weaknesses. Write them down. And then write down three ways that you could strengthen each one. This is a simple exercise that helps to promote clarity, from which a more concentrated sense of purpose emerges. And with this we are less affected by criticism and the fleeting opinions of others.

Opinions

As human beings we are primarily social-beings; thus our image of self can sometimes be influenced, to greater or lesser extent, by the opinions and judgements of other people: particularly those closest to us.

An important thing to remember here is not to internalise and depend upon these opinions, to the degree that they determine your sense of self-worth *at the core*. Yes of course, there are times when you may need to rely on the opinions of others, but just not to the point where those opinions determine your *overall* sense of esteem.

Let's say, for instance, that you run a small business and the opinions of your target market can contribute to the development of a product or service; then of course those opinions could be considered valuable and internalised for that purpose only. But not to the point where you begin doubting your own sense of self-worth, as a person, by questioning if *you* have what it takes to succeed. *Of course you do!*

> "Real and lasting self-worth does not come from the opinions of others."
>
> #TOOSYY

If we solely rely upon the opinions of others for our overall sense of self-worth then it is usually short lived. Real and lasting self-worth does not come from the opinions of others; but

among other things it can be cultivated from self-knowledge,
focused direction and purpose, a sense of accomplishment,
honesty, happiness, integrity, selfless contribution, self
inventory, and having a well defined list of *internal values*
(more on internal values later).

Overall, self-inventory is essential. This is where we take the
time to periodically look inward; objectively identifying our
strengths, weaknesses, natural abilities, character traits,
principles, our internal values and so forth.

The sense of self-worth which is gained from self-inventory is
not determined by the opinions of others. Instead, it is the result
of inner-stability. Without a strong sense of self-worth we
fluctuate from pole to pole, the ego becomes overinflated with
compliments or wilted with criticism.

This is particularly relevant to those of us *solely* concerned with
excessive people pleasing, and eliciting compliments from
others; because this type of worthiness is from the outside, in
(opinions and compliments of others); rather than from the
inside, out (inner stability).

To neutralise and overcome this we simply need to identify our
own strengths and weaknesses, likes and dislikes, natural talents,
and so on. This way we have surety within ourselves, but from
an internal perspective. We develop a firm inner-core,
unshakable by the opinions of others.

Whenever we incessantly worry about what others think of us, it
is the very act of doing so *in itself* which gives these external
factors their power. We surrender our sense of self-worth to the
opinions of others without realising that it is our own internal

judgements of them, which determine whether we value their opinion in the first place.

To put it another way; if we do not (consciously or unconsciously) put a person on some type of "pedestal," then we also lessen the tendency to use their opinions as the gauge with which we measure our own sense of self-worth. Think about that for a moment.

Friends & Relatives

As previously mentioned, friends and relatives—even associates—can also have the ability to affect the way we feel about ourselves. With this in mind it would be wise to carefully select those whose opinions you value. It may help to sit down with somebody that you feel can offer you an impartial view, and ask that person to write down what they would consider to be some of your character strengths.

Yes, this again is based on someone else's opinion but hopefully a more objective one. This may bring your awareness to an area, but whether you choose to accentuate and address it internally, or not, is your choice.

Once a few strengths have been keenly highlighted, you can repeat the exercise afterward—from a more empowered state— to perhaps identify any areas that may need development. After identifying these, and developing a strategy to overcome them, focus on the strengths again.

It's important to begin this exercise by noting the strengths first. You do not want to begin with the weaknesses and trigger off that internal voice of self-criticism, as this could then set an underlying theme of doubt toward the later mentioned strengths.

Again, for this exercise it's important that you approach the right person. Ask the wrong person for their objective opinion and you may end up with them projecting their own ideals and characteristics that they want to see in you. But this of course makes it a more biased opinion, rather than an impartial one.

The Scrambler

When do you feel most void of self-worth? Is it when you're around a certain person? Are there times when you wake up in the morning, look in the mirror and feel great; then as soon as you are around a certain person later that day (perhaps at work, etc.) you start to feel slightly unsure, as if your take on things suddenly holds less weight?

If the answer is yes to any of these then the solution is not rocket science; if possible, limit your time around those people.

However, perhaps you work with them or they are in your household, in which case they may not be so easily avoided. And maybe the associated feelings of inadequacy are triggered because you feel as though they purposely undermine you. But still, ultimately, how you see that person is your own creation because it is the result of your own *internal representation* of them (how you see them in your mind's eye).

Here's a light-hearted and simple visualisation exercise— sometimes used within the field of Neuro-Linguistic Programming—that may help to take the seriousness (and therefore the perceived threat) out of the situation; stay with me:

1. First of all, call this person to mind and imagine what your next encounter with them might be like. Vividly imagine dealing with them at some point in the near future.

2. I would assume that you now have quite a clear picture of this person in mind. So, how do you see them in this mental picture? And how does it make you feel?

3. Imagine for a moment if this picture was real, which element of it would make you feel most uncomfortable?

4. For instance, in this mental image, is this person larger than you for instance? Do they have a loud or deep voice, or a piercing look on their face? Which elements do you find most uncomfortable?

5. When you notice which elements of this mental image are slightly overinflated within your imagination, first let's begin to make them "normal" again. For example, if you imagine them as being taller than they actually are, then shrink them down to the right size. Or if their voice is unreasonably loud or irritating, as you imagine your encounter; then turn it down. One by one, change all of the accentuated elements of this mental image to make it more normal.

6. Now, what we are going to do is change some of the content in that mental image and make it unrealistic again, but this time we are going to do it, *our way*.

7. Concentrate on their face for a moment; now imagine what they would look like with a big red clown's nose, yes that's right, I said it; a big red clown's nose.

8. How about if you add a clown's hat as well, why not just add a full clown outfit while you're at it. If you're someone that has a phobia of clowns, then use something else that you would deem equally ludicrous.

Now, how does that make this person seem? Rather ridiculous right? In your mind's eye, do they seem quite so difficult to deal with now? Are you taking them as seriously? More importantly, does the thought of dealing with them make you feel annoyed or as disempowered as you may have done prior?

So, what exactly are we doing here? Really it's quite simple; we are changing how we view this person in our minds eye; as it is only ever here that they become larger than life. If we constantly change how we see them internally, this will begin to scramble any negative feelings triggered by thinking about that person.

Within the imagination, our worries and concerns are often blown out of proportion as they tend to seem worse than they actually are, and this is why we are manipulating this image here, within the mind's eye *first*.

Prior to a title fight, if a boxer imagined himself being knocked out by his opponent, how do you think this would affect his morale? And if he envisioned it vice versa, again, how would *this* affect his morale? Although pre-fight, either one of these *mental images* could affect his performance and influence the outcome. In fact, as we'll see in the next chapter, mental imagery can make all the difference.

We have the power to determine how we feel when in the presence of others by changing how we internally represent them (how we see them in our mind's eye).

If you view someone as arrogant then you are more likely to see those traits in everything they do. If that person were displaying genuine confidence you'd probably still label it arrogance, accustomed to viewing them through those "lenses."

Imagine wearing a pair of sunglasses with blue lenses; of course the entire world would look blue. But would that mean that everything in the world was *actually* blue? Likewise when viewing someone (or something) in a certain way we usually become biased by that viewpoint. *"People don't see things how they are, people see things how THEY are."*

The Scrambler can also work with most memories where the image is one that bothers you. Changing the content, especially in humorous and ridiculous ways, can totally shift how a negative memory makes us feel, along with how we view a current situation.

In a way it's similar to the common "naked audience" technique that is used by some inexperienced speakers when their nerves have got the better of them. If a nervous speaker is to give a presentation in front of a considerably large crowd, they might imagine the people in the audience are sitting there in their underwear.

As ridiculous as it sounds this can actually have a couple of benefits for the nervous speaker: it distracts them from thinking thoughts of failure and it makes light of the situation. The inexperienced speaker can then give their presentation, while distracted from self consciousness and criticism.

Although seemingly quirky, these simple techniques can actually be quite effective when used to divert our imagination from dwelling on needless worries or blowing things out of proportion. "Don't knock it until you try it."

Self Inventory

As we saw earlier; a crucial part of self inventory is writing down your strengths and weaknesses objectively. This can be absolutely essential when building self-worth providing that there is not too much focus on the negatives, as this may instigate unnecessary self-criticism.

Remember a time/place when/where you felt whole and complete as a person. In fact don't just remember it, relive it vividly in your mind.

Focus only on the positive feelings that you felt at the time. What was your key strength here? Perhaps it was confidence, poise, or even humour; whatever it was, immediately write it down.

If you cannot recall such a time, then think of something that you really enjoy doing, you may notice some character strengths that you posses in that area. Ultimately, you are looking for some key attributes of your character that you can write down.

"*Write down? How boring,*" you might say. Yes, boring it may be at first, but in writing these attributes down and looking at them frequently; your written words will serve as powerful visual reminders if you ever catch yourself slipping; that is to say, doubting your ability.

To accentuate these strengths even further, first thing tomorrow morning look yourself in the eye, in the mirror, and tell yourself, audibly, how much you sincerely appreciate these strengths and what you can accomplish with them. When I first started out, this is something that I would do every morning without fail.

I even used to show appreciation for my weaknesses, as they too only motivated me to become stronger, by conquering them. If everything were to be perfect, there would be little opportunity to grow mentally and spiritually.

Positive Morning Ritual

The word Ritual is defined as: *"A series of actions performed, according to a prescribed order."* Therefore, a *Morning Ritual* is simply a set of particular actions that you habitually perform every morning. And this can, of course, have an impact on the rest of your day.

However, most of us don't have a positive morning ritual. Instead, we begin the day by responding to the demands of others; whether that means checking emails, messengers, social networks, and so forth.

And on top of that, many people then do one of the worst things that a person can do, in the morning, to positively influence their day: they watch the News and/or read the Newspapers.

Doing so is logical if your line of work depends on you being aptly informed on all sorts of current events (a radio presenter perhaps), or maybe you might want to check the stock markets or the Public Notices section of the newspaper and nothing else. But if you are more interested in the stories they have to offer, your time could probably be much better spent.

Rarely do we see stories of empowerment (and they *are* out there) broadcasted on the mainstream News networks. Furthermore, many of the News (programmes/papers) tend to primarily accentuate what's "wrong" with the world, and this is simply because negativity—playing on people's curiosity—sells.

However; subscribing to such negativity, especially first thing in the morning, increases the chance that you will then (consciously or unconsciously) go through the entire day in the associated mindset.

Instead, why not develop a *Positive Morning Ritual* (an empowering set of actions) that will set you up with a mindset of positivity and empowerment throughout the day? That way, even if you do experience any negativity, it will have less of an effect.

You could use the morning ritual that I'm about to describe, inspired by Stefan Pylarinos (6) and Tony Robbins (7), or simply create your own; whatever works for you. Either way, the first thing you could do when you wake up is:

Smile: Instead of waking up and thinking, "Oh, here we go again, another day." Wake up and immediately smile. A smile can work wonders for our mindset. Give thanks that you have woken up to see another day; many others were not as fortunate (more on smiling later on in this chapter).

Stretch: After hours of being in the same position the muscles within the body need to "wake up" and energise. Besides this; not only is stretching considered to be natures very own method of distributing vital life-force (known within eastern philosophy as Chi, Ki, Orgone or Prana) throughout the nervous system, but also, by stretching you release endorphins from the brain and these help to create a positive mood, automatically helping to boost your sense of self-worth.

Deep Breaths: Breathing exercises are often one of the most overlooked remedies for combating stress and anxiety. Taking some slow deep breaths can help to normalize the blood pressure, sharpen our focus by providing increased oxygen to the brain, regulate the heart rate, and loosen up the muscles.

In addition to this, deep breathing also cleanses the respiratory system while promoting increased stimulation of the Pituitary and Limbic systems which release hormones that make us feel good.

Drink a cup of water: Of course, after many hours rest the body can become dehydrated. Drinking a cup of (room temperature, or warm) water not only replenishes your reserves, but the hydration alone will stimulate your body to wake up quicker.

If you are a "slow starter" in the morning, then this could be more due to dehydration than anything else. Yet to remedy this, many of us will go and make a cup of Tea or Coffee for a fix of caffeine, which over time can dehydrate the body even more. Water is your best bet, natures very own elixir.

According to research conducted by the Japanese Medical Society, drinking water first thing in the morning—at least 45 minutes before eating—can also help to prevent or cure the following conditions: headache, body-ache, arthritis, epilepsy, excess fatness, bronchitis, asthma, TB, meningitis, kidney and urine infections, vomiting, gastritis, diarrhoea, piles, diabetes, constipation, eye infections, womb cancer and menstrual disorders; along with many ear, nose and throat diseases.

After smiling, stretching, taking some deep breaths and drinking water; you could also do 20-to-30 light Star Jumps (Jumping Jacks). This helps to stimulate the blood circulation around the body and also releases even more endorphins.

And while doing these Star Jumps; you can say, out loud, all of the character strengths (that you noted down earlier) which you are grateful for. You can also use some of the one-liner affirmations at the back of this book. This will promote a positive outlook toward yourself (self-worth) and the day ahead.

Although this may initially look like a lot to do—in writing, it only looks as such because I am explaining the benefits of each step as we go along. In actuality this entire sequence will take you less than 5 minutes.

After you have completed these five simple steps, you could then take another few minutes to *positively* answer some of the following questions:

What am I happy about in my life right now?

e.g. "I am happy that I'm alive; I am happy that I am healthy; I am happy that I am reading this book and developing myself; my children make me happy," etc.

How does that make me feel?

e.g. "This makes me feel as though I am *on purpose*; this makes me feel fulfilled; this makes me feel truly grateful to my creator," etc.

What am I excited about right now?

e.g. "I am excited that I am taking my personal development to the next level; I am excited about all the opportunities that are available to me at this very moment; I am excited about creating my life to order," etc.

What am I proud of in my life?

e.g. "I am proud that I have made it this far in my life; I am proud of myself for not quitting on myself; I am proud of my contributions toward the betterment of others and the planet, I am proud of my accomplishments to date; I am proud of my children," etc.

What am I passionate about in my life?

e.g. "I am passionate about *becoming more;* I am passionate about contributing to the betterment of the world; I am passionate about providing the best life for my family and loved ones; I am passionate about being the best that I can possibly be," etc.

What am I enjoying right now in my life?

e.g. "I am enjoying learning; I enjoy becoming stronger and wiser as a person; I enjoy helping others to realise their potential; I am enjoying this book; I enjoy my hobbies and

interests; I enjoy spending time with my children and helping
them to develop; I am enjoying the process of becoming
financially free," etc.

<u>What am I committed to right now in my life?</u>

e.g. "I am committed to all of the above; I am committed to
doing my positive morning ritual which will positively impact
my day; I am committed to taking action on some of the things
that I have learnt from reading this book; I am committed to
raising my standards and not living a run-of-the-mill life," etc.

<u>Who/what do I love?</u>

e.g. "I love my creator; I love nature; I love me, I love life, I
love my children; I love my parents; I love my family and close
friends, I love my pets," etc.

<u>Who loves me?</u>

e.g. "My creator loves me; my family and close friends love me;
my children love me; my spouse loves me; my pets love me,"
etc.

<u>What am I grateful for?</u>

e.g. "I am eternally grateful to my creator; I am grateful to be
alive, I am grateful for the air that I breathe; I am grateful for the
food that I eat and the water I drink; I am grateful for my good
health; I am grateful for the power of the mind; I am grateful for
my powerful immune system; I am grateful to the Sun for
sustaining life on this planet; I am grateful for the Atoms that
sustain the physical world," etc.

Of course, the answers above are illustrative; they are not necessarily *the* answers. Your answers should be honest in accordance with *your* life. Some of them may be the same as those above, some may differ.

Either way, once you begin to implement your own positive morning ritual into your daily routine, I guarantee that you will begin to have even more of an optimistic view on life. Opportunities will arise that you may not have noticed before, and life will generally seem more fulfilling and rewarding.

> "The more that you are grateful for; the more that things will manifest into your life for you to be grateful for: like attracts like!"
>
> #TOOSYY

This is because a positive morning ritual will stimulate an "Attitude of Gratitude," and the more that you are grateful for; the more that things will manifest into your life for you to be grateful for: like attracts like!

As you can see by some of the foregoing examples, there is no shortage of things to be happy or grateful for. It simply takes for us to turn our attention toward those things (the word "things" being used loosely) and this is particularly beneficial to do in the morning as it provides the undertone for the rest of the day.

If you are then later confronted with some negative news, it will be more readily neutralised. Oftentimes; *how you start the day, is how you end the day.*

Again, although I have explained the positive morning ritual in some depth here, do not be put off by the detail; you can have the *whole* sequence completed within 10-to-15 minutes, or perhaps it may take slightly longer if you decide to add in some meditation and/or chanting time.

What you do, or how long you take, is not the point here. The point is: *get started.* Tailor it how you wish. Either way it will begin to enable you to see the bigger picture and increase your sense of self-worth in the process.

The Whole Picture

Right now, get up and walk to the nearest picture on your wall, get as close as you possibly can to that picture, even until your nose is touching it. Now say out loud what you can see in that picture.

Once you have done this, take a giant step back and notice if the picture makes more sense from that view? Of course it does! Our focus of the picture is blurred if we are standing to close to it.

Self inventory, positive morning rituals, writing down our key abilities, so on and so forth, can all help us to take a step back from the "picture." From this vantage point we gain a wider view of our lives, and our capabilities. We can still pay keen attention to detail but just from a more broadened perspective.

Just Do It

As we covered within the first cornerstone of this book; you also get a strong sense of self-worth when you are sure that you have achieved something. You may not experience this unless you are doing just that: *achieving*.

Have you ever prolonged something and then finally got around to doing it? If so, afterwards, did you feel much better and even somewhat accomplished; as if a slight weight was off your shoulders? Did you think; "Why didn't I just do this age's ago?" Be honest; you know you did.

When you want to do something that is fully within your power to do—something that you know needs addressing—*just do it.* Thinking about all of the "why's and wherefores" only allows room for doubt, inertia and excuses to join the process.

Integrity is also essential for cultivating self-worth. Stick to your word. If you say you're going to do something, then do it. Your word is your bond.

The more that you stick to your word, the more powerful your word becomes; thus if you say it, *then it's going to happen.* On the other hand, the more that we say we are going to do something and don't carry it out, the more we are weakening our willpower and integrity.

We also weaken our sense of commitment, reliability, and our self-worth. Remember, exercising these traits is just like exercising any other skill or ability: *if you don't use it, you lose it.*

Positive Contributions

We are all on this planet to contribute in some way. This doesn't necessarily mean financially; it could be time, knowledge, wisdom, skill sets, advice, expertise, love, a smile, a listening ear, so on and so forth.

Sincerely contributing toward something, without expecting anything in return is the highest form of generosity, it automatically makes us feel more worthy within ourselves.

It could be seen as though each of us has a kind of internal contribution-meter; which we use to consciously, or unconsciously, measure the balance of "give and take" that exists within our relationships. But the person who just takes and takes, without ever selflessly contributing, is essentially violating this basic principle of reciprocal balance.

> ## "Self-worthiness is promoted through altruistic contribution."
> #TOOSYY

Self-worthiness is promoted through altruistic contribution. It is one of the reasons that some of us feel compelled to donate millions of pounds to charities, and others of us may donate our time, love, expertise and so forth.

As, Zig Ziglar once said, *"If you help enough people get what they want, then you automatically get what you want."*

Also, on the topic of contribution, go ahead and contribute more to life itself; *get involved more,* become more of a contributor on the playing field, rather than a spectator at the sidelines.

Smile

Please, please, please, never underestimate the power of a smile. Smile more often and you may be surprised with the changes that occur within your life. Opportunities will present themselves when we become more approachable and this, in itself, can contribute to how we feel about ourselves.

I am not saying we wear a permanent kind of cheesy smile, which is tasteless from a mile off, I am simply suggesting that smiling more will not only have a positive impact upon how we view ourselves and the world around us, but also upon how others perceive us.

In his article: *Top Ten Reasons to Smile* (8), Mark Stibich, Ph.D., lists ten reasons why smiling is beneficial to us, and they are as follows:

1. "Smiling makes us attractive"

"We are naturally drawn to people who smile. There is an attraction factor. We want to know a smiling person and figure out what is so good. Frowns, scowls and grimaces all push people away—but a smile draws them in."

2. "Smiling changes our mood"

"Next time you are feeling down, try putting on a smile. There's a good chance that your mood will change for the better. Smiling can trick the body into helping you change your mood."

3. "Smiling is contagious"

"When someone is smiling they lighten up the room, change the moods of others, and make things happier. A smiling person brings happiness with them. Smile a lot and you will draw people to you."

4. "Smiling relieves stress"

"Stress can really show up in our faces. Smiling helps to prevent us from looking tired, worn down, and overwhelmed. When you are stressed, take time to put on a smile. The stress should be reduced and you'll be better able to take action."

5. "Smiling boosts your immune system"

"Smiling helps the immune system to work better. When you smile, immune function improves possibly because you are more relaxed. Prevent the flu and colds by smiling."

6. "Smiling lowers your blood pressure"

"When you smile, there is a measurable reduction in your blood pressure. Give it a try if you have a blood pressure monitor at home. Sit for a few minutes, take a reading. Then smile for a minute and take another reading while still smiling. Do you notice a difference?"

7. "Smiling releases endorphins, natural pain killers and serotonin"

"Studies have shown that smiling releases endorphins, natural pain killers, and serotonin. Together these three make us feel good. Smiling is a natural drug."

8. "Smiling lifts the face and makes you look younger"

"The muscles we use to smile lift the face, making a person appear younger. Don't go for a face lift, just try smiling your way through the day — you'll look younger and feel better."

9. "Smiling makes you seem successful"

"Smiling people appear more confident, are more likely to be promoted, and more likely to be approached. Put on a smile at meetings and appointments and people will react to you differently."

10. "Smiling helps you stay positive"

"Try this test: Smile. Now try to think of something negative without losing the smile. It's hard. When we smile our body is sending the rest of us a message that "life is good!" Stay away from depression, stress and worry by smiling."

Following on from this, we also begin to loosen up a little when we smile and, as a result, we view ourselves less critically.

Sometimes, the more seriously we take ourselves the more we engage in negative self-criticism, and this is especially true if we lack a well defined set of internal values.

Although heightened self-worth can be *cultivated* by many of the ideas and strategies shared throughout this chapter, it is also *underpinned* by our internal values.

Internal Values

Our *internal* values are our innermost values. They are a reflection of what we deem most important to us.

When our values are based on principles such as: love, truth, justice, honour, integrity, loyalty, service to others, interdependence, self development and so forth; they provide us with a strong and enduring sense of self-worth because they are in harmony with the progressive principles of nature.

However, if our highest values are derived from (and attached to) the transient things of this world such as: material possessions, titles, habitual pleasure seeking, social or professional status, and so forth; then our sense of self-worth and identity fluctuates with these external factors and is forevermore at the mercy of them.

In the event that these superficial things are then taken away, their absence quickly re-exposes the gap in our identity that we were relying upon them to conceal. This gap is the void. Our sense of self-worth is then exposed to the elements as we are easily blown about by the winds of life with no real grounding.

Deep rooted and lasting self worth is often the *fruit* of our own positive internal values, grown upon the *tree* of correct knowledge, with the foundation being rooted within the fertile *soil* of timeless principles that exist throughout nature; being those which are in sync with growth, progression, expansion, and so forth.

As per the common saying: *"We either stand for something or fall for anything."* And it's our innermost *values* that define what we stand for. Heightened self-worth comes naturally when we are living our lives in accordance with these values; and to gain maximum clarity, just as we did with our strengths and weaknesses earlier, it may help to specifically identify them by writing them down.

Once we have identified, and written down, our internal values we become more focused and resolute toward our path: *we stand for something*. These values are like the compass that we use to provide direction and guidance, without this compass we inevitably lack direction and become increasingly prone to temptation: *we fall for anything*.

Without a clear list of values from which we can derive our self-worth it becomes increasingly challenging to subordinate the pleasures of the moment to our overall purpose, and this is because we become short sighted to the things that matter most. In the words of, Stephen Covey: "The main thing is to *keep* the main thing, the *main* thing."

Some people, when questioned on their values, might say that they already know what they stand for; and to some degree they probably do. However, the main question here is: are your highest values attached to those transient things we mentioned earlier? Or are they centred on principles that will provide a solid foundation for your personal growth, developing you internally?

Furthermore, if I were to ask you: *"What are your internal values?"* Would you have a clearly defined list? For example; perhaps you base your highest values on qualities such as: honesty, justice, trust, loyalty, full self expression, personal development, being a good role model, leading by example, empathy, positive contribution to others, respect for nature, pro-activity, the development of any dependents, and so forth.

However, if you haven't given this much thought until this point, then you might want to take a moment to answer the following questions:

1. What are the foremost principles and values that you look for in others? (These will often be the attributes that you value most)

2. What values (or attributes) will you absolutely *not* compromise on?

3. What virtues (or legacy) would you want to be remembered for once your time in the physical realm expires?

The answers to these questions will bring additional clarity to your internal values. Once you have taken some time to honestly and thoughtfully answer them, write down a list of the top eight internal values which you would deem most important.

Once you have your top eight, now imagine you were forced to reduce that number by half; which four would you keep, and why? Now finally, if you had to pick just *one* out of those four as your most important internal value, which one would it be?

Once you have identified your single highest value, you will find a fundamental source of strength and stability. This will become a significant part of the *unshakable core* mentioned earlier. And as long as you stay true to it, your sense of self-worth will be maintained throughout the toughest of adversity.

Real Worthiness

Self-worth cannot *truly* be cultivated without first clearly identifying your *internal values*. It is simply not possible to measure *real* worthiness, without first having a *cause* to be worthy of.

Your internal values are a reflection of that cause. They are the offspring of the principles most important to you, and once you clarify these it becomes easier to stay on the correct path.

Now that we have taken a look into *self-worth* and the essential role it plays toward us *becoming more* internally; we can expand further within this area and take a look at a quality that is also closely related. In fact it is so closely related to self-worth that the two are often used interchangeably to describe the same attribute: some might even say it's almost like "splitting hairs."

Nonetheless, along with self-worth, it's also a key attribute to cultivate from within, because just like self-worth if we rely solely upon the opinions of others to generate it, then it's seldom long lasting. And that attribute is…

Chapter 6

CONFIDENCE

"With confidence, you have won before you have even started." – Marcus Garvey

Although very closely related, self-confidence and self-worth are not the same in entirety. Nonetheless, they are both respectively essential on our quest toward *becoming more*.

As we have seen, our level of self-worth is generally an overall assessment of how we feel toward ourselves, encompassing: our morals, principles, habits, strengths, weaknesses, appearance, accomplishments, and so on. Conversely, self-confidence can sometimes be used to describe the level of surety that we have in our ability to perform a *certain* task. Some people may even refer to this, in certain contexts, as self efficacy.

"Competence equals confidence."
#TOOSYY

For instance; if someone were a professional builder, they could of course be *confident* (strongly certain) in their ability to build a small house from scratch within, say, six months. Within this area, their competence would generate self-confidence. However, this does not necessarily mean that the same individual would value themselves *overall* as a person, or indeed their life's higher purpose for that matter.

Although someone who has a high sense of self-worth may be likely to possess a natural air of self-confidence, the same cannot always be said contrariwise. Again, someone can be confident within themselves relating to particular areas, but still not respect, like, love, trust, care-for, or believe in themselves, overall.

Just as many of the catalysts for low self-worth can also be the causes of low self-confidence, most of the strategies used for building self-worth can also be applied for building self-confidence and vice versa.

Throughout this chapter you will find some of the many techniques which can be used to develop and maintain self-confidence. And if they are applied with consistency they will improve your results in this area. As a result, they will also inspire you to take on new challenges with enhanced optimism.

The first three techniques that we're going to take a look at can be used to elicit self-confident states at will. They are basic exercises, commonly used by some NLP practitioners, which can assist individuals to empower themselves. I am availing them here so now *you* can also use them to empower yourself, if you wish to do so.

The remaining strategies which follow on from the first three are more related to subtle lifestyle changes, and these will also accentuate and promote heightened self-confidence. With no further ado, the first of these techniques is:

Anchoring

Anchoring (9) is a technique that is most commonly associated with the late Russian Psychologist, Ivan Pavlov. Pavlov is nowadays most commonly known for his research in the area of "Conditioned Reflexes (10)" also known as "Classical Conditioning" (11).

It was while researching this that he conducted many studies, one of the most famous of which being in the year 1901. This study later became known as "Pavlov's Dogs." The technique was very simple, but still highly effective.

So what did Pavlov do? He noticed that every time he fed his dogs they would salivate at the sight of the food which, of course, is fairly straightforward. However, it was what he did next that made it a *conditioned* reflex.

Pavlov simply rang a bell every time he would feed his dogs. And as he began to consistently repeat this, of course the dogs naturally began to associate the ringing of the bell with food. Even when Pavlov rang the bell, with no food, the dogs would still salivate at the sound of the bell alone.

This was a *conditioned reflex*; Pavlov had conditioned the dogs to salivate at the sound of the bell rather than at the sight of the food. And he had done this by repeatedly associating a stimulus (the bell) with a state (hunger). And this later became known as *anchoring*.

It is a technique so widely used in the advertising world that it has become common place. Can you tell which product that this phrase is anchored to; "Have a break, have a...?"

If you said Kit Kat, you are absolutely correct. For many of us, the phrase alone immediately produces the corresponding mental image of the chocolate bar.

A similar form of anchoring is also commonly used in adverts which elicit particular emotional responses, i.e. laughter or even sympathy. At the exact moment during the advert that we are laughing or sympathising, the advertiser will usually show whatever product they are promoting.

The idea here is that the image of the product will become neurologically linked with these feelings of happiness or sympathy, for happiness triggers positivity; and sympathy, well, increased susceptibility (defencelessness).

Then at a later date when we see that product on the supermarket shelf it may unconsciously trigger these emotional states, causing the unsuspecting consumer to be more inclined to buy that product over another brand, even if it costs slightly more. Of course, happiness and sympathy are just two of many emotions which are used.

The same method of anchoring (association) is also used to link "superstars" or attractive people to certain products via advertising. That said; anchoring is only one of many techniques used by savvy advertising agencies; and a rather basic one at that.

OK, OK, I know; you want the point right? The point here is that anchors can obviously be used as powerful stimuli that bring about certain states of mind—thoughts and emotions. And this is because memory works on the principle of association.

How does that relate to self confidence? Quite simply, because if you were to vividly and repeatedly relive a certain memory—of a time that you felt totally self-confident—then as you were doing so you would also begin to (emotionally) elicit the same state of confidence which you had on that occasion.

Now, if every time you vividly educed that memory you repeatedly touched the knuckle of your left pinkie finger; pretty soon if you were to touch that knuckle (the stimulus) in exactly the same way as you did when reliving the memory, it would trigger the empowered state of confidence associated with the memory. In this case you would have *conditioned* a simple touch of the pinkie finger to elicit the emotional state of confidence.

This is called *a voluntary anchor,* as you are consciously setting it up. However some anchors are set *unconsciously* and these are *involuntary anchors.* For an example of the latter, can you remember a time when you split up with an ex partner, and throughout that time you may have listened to a certain song repeatedly?

You may not have realised it at the time, but *you were anchoring that song to the corresponding emotional state.* If you heard that song at a later date, how did it make you feel? In addition to this, the forthcoming statement may be worth some consideration: Many of these involuntary anchors can also work without us even being aware of the triggers.

Put simply, an anchor is any stimulus that evokes a specific conditioned (emotional or mental) state in someone. So how do we establish our own voluntary anchors that work to our benefit? For the purpose of this exercise we are going to focus on what is sometimes referred to as *Tactile Anchoring*, and this means anchoring through the use of touch.

First off, pick a part of your body that you wish to use as the stimulus (or trigger) for the anchor. This could be a certain place on your hand, your arm or perhaps even your thigh, as long as it is easily accessible if you need to use it.

Setting the stimulus, for a confidence anchor, on somewhere like your ankle may not be convenient if you need to use it in public—perhaps before giving a speech or presentation—unless of course, you wish to stand like a pigeon on one leg while you trigger it.

It is also important for the stimulus to be on a part of the body which is not too frequently touched otherwise. For example setting it on the palm of your hand wouldn't particularly be the best place. This is because we often hold things in the palm of our hands and the stimulus could often be triggered unnecessarily and quickly lose its uniqueness and potency. It would be best to pick somewhere that is not often touched unless you wish to "fire your anchor."

Many people use the knuckle of their pinkie finger. Others may use an earlobe, or any other part of the body which is infrequently touched but still easily accessible. When you are applying the anchor it is also important that you touch the stimulus (say, your pinkie finger) in a very specific way; and the same way every single time.

Now we have that bit out of the way, let's look at getting into the state (the emotional state) that you wish to draw upon at will, this is called *The Resource State*.

So firstly, let's get into that empowering and confidently positive state. (Note: for simplicity, while explaining this exercise I will assume that you are using your left pinkie finger knuckle as the stimulus.)

1. Can you remember a time when you were doing something which you really love to do (your favourite hobby perhaps)?

2. Now, what is it that you *really* love about doing that thing? And how confident and positive do you feel when you are engaged in this activity?

3. Really take a moment to focus intensely on how confident and positive you feel.

4. It is important that you become really associated with this feeling as if you were engaged in the activity right now. Once you are familiar with these steps (1-to-4), you might find it easier to close your eyes throughout this part of the exercise.

5. When you notice that confident and positive state beginning to peak, *this is your resource state.* Now apply the stimulus by touching your left pinkie finger knuckle in a specific way (i.e. maybe you tap it repeatedly, or hold it down continually with a certain level of pressure). You want to do this *just* before you feel your empowering and confident state reaching its peak.

6. As soon as you feel the state beginning to dwindle release the anchor immediately. You only want to anchor the peak state, and *not* the dwindling state. When

initially setting up your anchor, the stimulus should be applied for anywhere between 5-to-15 seconds. This means that you link the empowering state (self confidence, positivity, etc.) to the stimulus (pinkie finger) for anywhere between that time. This will ensure you get the very peak of the state you are anchoring.

7. Once you have completed steps 1 through to 6, stop and think of something else for 10-to-20 seconds to clear your mind. Now repeat steps 1 through to 6 again. Make sure that the trigger/stimulus (i.e. tapping the pinkie finger) is applied in exactly the same way as before. Now, again, stop and clear your mind for a moment. Repeat this entire process 5-to-8 times.

8. Now we are going to test the anchor. Imagine a situation happening in the future where you might not have been so confident before. For example, if you are not a confident public speaker you could imagine a scenario of having to give a speech in public. As soon as you begin to feel those feelings associated with lack of confidence, *then trigger your anchor.* Touch your left pinkie finger in the exact same place and in the exact same way that you did when setting up the anchor in the first place. How does it feel? Does the empowering and confident state of the anchor overcome, or at least neutralise, the less confident state? If so great, you have set a successful anchor; if not then your resource state (the empowering state you were eliciting) may not have been intense enough while setting the anchor. In this case be sure to elicit a stronger resource state (whether through memory

or even by just using your imagination) and set another anchor.

9. Trigger the anchor the next day to ensure it has been well set, and that it is lasting.

Some Key Points to remember

I. Anchoring works by linking things together neurologically and this is what makes it so powerful.

II. The anchor should be applied for anywhere between 5-to-15 seconds at a time.

III. The anchor should be triggered in exactly the same way every time you link it to the empowering and confident state, and when setting it off.

IV. When initially setting the anchor, begin doing so just as you are reaching the high point of the empowered resource state.

V. When testing out your anchor, if the resource state is not powerful enough and you are continuing to feel anxiety from the imagined scenario that you are not confident in, then stop applying the anchor immediately! Otherwise, you may anchor the negative state.

VI. You can strengthen the anchor by repeating steps 1-to-6 (for setting it up) over several days.

VII. If you experience a situation where you are really confident, or you are actually physically doing that hobby which you love to do; if possible, you can also set up your anchor in real-time to capture that empowering state too.

The Circle of Excellence

Another simple and effective technique to increase self-confidence is known as "The circle of excellence."

Now, this technique may not create competence in the skill you desire, meaning, you won't suddenly become highly skilled at a physical task without having to practice. But instead, the circle of excellence helps to create the requisite self-confidence for us to take action in a particular area.

For instance; if you had a fear of public speaking (my favourite example), this technique will by no means render you the most seasoned of speakers overnight. But, it will increase the self-confidence that is necessary to get up there and get the job done.

Here are the steps for using the circle of excellence which, like anchoring, you will need to set up ahead of time:

1. Close your eyes and imagine an empty circle on the floor. In your imagination, make it big enough for you to comfortably step into it, but imagine it at least one foot out in front of you (note: when first starting out, you could keep your eyes open and draw a circle on the floor with chalk).

2. Next, remember a time when you were absolutely empowered and confident. A time where you were flawless at what you were doing, everything went smoothly; you were immeasurably bright, funny, happy,

confident, fearless and completely full of energy. You were completely balanced, creative and radiantly powerful, or any other empowering trait that you wish to add. This doesn't have to be a major accomplishment; it could be something as simple as a small hobby, or anything else where you experience any of the above feelings. Be fully associated with this state, (meaning; in the memory you are looking through your own eyes and not through the eyes of a third party) fully experiencing the feelings.

3. Now imagine yourself putting all of those empowering feelings into the circle in front of you, one by one. You are beginning to fill the circle with your confidence, your fearlessness, your charisma, and so on. That is your *circle of excellence*. Visualise it intensely, picture that circle being full of life, it now has all the vibrant energy (and/or colour) inside it from these empowering states.

4. Now, when these feelings are at their peak, step into your circle. Intensify them even more. Feel the powerful emotion surrounding you and flowing through your body. Enjoy the associated feeling and become totally one with it; and once you're done, step outside the circle.

5. Now visualise yourself folding up the circle with all of the powerful states still inside, and perhaps putting it in your pocket to carry around; or whatever works for you.

You can now use your circle of excellence whenever you need it. For example, if you were nervous about giving a presentation; just as you were walking up to begin, in your mind's eye, you could throw your circle down on the floor in front of you, where you are about to stand and give your presentation.

You could then simply step into this imaginary circle as you begin the presentation. This simple technique will then trigger the state that you experienced when you set it up initially.

Note: If you cannot recall a time where you felt really empowered and confident, then use your imagination. Imagine yourself as being confident, assertive, unstoppable and powerful, and when you have that feeling, anchor it to your circle.

The reason that you can use your imagination here is because the human *nervous system* (which plays a key role in determining your emotional state) cannot differentiate between a memory and an imagined scenario; nor can it differentiate between either of these, and a real experience. This is evidenced by the technique known as *Mental Imagery* commonly used by athletes.

Mental Imagery can boost our competence in a skill by employing the imagination alone. For instance, if you were to imagine yourself performing a certain task to perfection, while doing this you would be stimulating specific neurological patterns within the brain.

However, the same neurological patterns would also be stimulated whether you were physically performing the action, imagining it, or recalling the memory thereof (more on this in the next chapter). So go ahead, get fully associated with your desired state and set up your *circle of excellence.*

The Swish Pattern

The Swish pattern is a type of visualisation exercise that can be particularly useful for replacing certain types of unwanted behavioural patterns, with new and empowering alternatives.

You may want to first read through the basic steps of this technique to familiarise yourself with the process. You can then practice it without reading the instructions as this will allow you to flow more smoothly.

Now; say, for instance, that you are someone who tends to feel a little withdrawn (shy or timid) when first meeting new people or visiting new environments.

Perhaps you want to, instead, replace this with an attitude of confidence and assertiveness but—due to low willpower—every time that you try to do so you still find yourself reverting back to the old pattern.

To help remedy this by using the Swish Pattern, when you have some quiet time alone, first you need to:

1. Close your eyes and imagine a *large red blank* movie screen.

2. Now, on that movie screen, begin to imagine yourself in an environment being surrounded by new people; and notice yourself exhibiting this unwanted shy and timid type of behaviour.

3. Next in the bottom right hand corner visualise a small screen with a *green background,* and on that screen picture yourself looking and feeling exceptionally

confident; stood confidently, talking confidently, not forced confidence but calm genuine inner confidence. On the green screen, picture yourself confidently mingling and networking with new people.

4. At this point you are simultaneously visualising two screens: one being the big main screen with the *red* background (displaying you as shy), and the other being a small screen in the bottom right hand corner with a *green* background (displaying you as confident) .

5. Now take your right hand and imagine that you are slowly bringing the smaller (green screen) picture closer to you, imagine it becoming bigger and bigger, as you move it closer, until it becomes so close to you that it breaks through the picture on the red screen, completely replacing it.

6. You can now see the new *confident you* in the main screen. And the old image on the red screen has shattered and completely disappeared.

    (Side Note: Just as the smaller picture of the *empowered you* breaks through onto the main screen, some people tend to find it more effective if they make an audible whoosh, or swish sound hence the name, *Swish Pattern.* However, the sound itself is not particularly important, but the image and the speed at which it breaks through, are.)

7. Once you have done this, you will need to momentarily pause and open your eyes for a second. This is called "breaking state".

8. Now repeat steps 1 through to 7 again: see the old "timid you" with the red background as the main picture, and see the new "confident you" with the green background as the small picture in the bottom right hand corner. Again, use your right hand and bring the smaller picture closer until it bursts through the big picture and becomes the main screen, "whoosh;" then break state.

9. You can start off slowly to get familiar with the process, but once familiar, begin to make each swish pattern (transition between pictures) increasingly quicker.

   (Side Note: Once you have completed each swish; *always break state in-between the patterns!* If you do not do this you will be simply looping the positive state back into the negative one, which will completely defeat the purpose.)

10. Repeat the swish pattern at least 5-to-10 times (sometimes more may be required). Each time the picture-transition process should be done more rapidly: opening your eyes for a second or two in-between each one.

11. After you have completed a few repetitions of this exercise, I guarantee it would be hard to visualise the image of the old shy version of you. This is because the picture in your head will automatically change to the new confident version of you.

So what exactly are we doing here? It's really quite simple: we are setting a new mental pattern.

If I were to think of myself giving a speech, and within that thought I pictured myself as being incompetent; then there would be a fairly good chance of me actually behaving this way, when delivering my speech.

However, if I re-programme my brain (as in my neurological connections) to replace that image whenever it arises with a new empowered and confident image of me; then consequently, in the same situation, I am more likely to behave in that confident manner while giving my speech.

After repeating the swish pattern, as many times as necessary, we now have a new pattern whereby the brain will swiftly, and automatically, switch the disempowering thought (of timidity) to its empowering alternative (confidence).

Instead of the old pattern: visualising failure (what if I fail?), we are "rewiring" that thought process into one of success (I can easily do this).

Utilising this simple technique is merely one way that we can instigate new and empowering neurological patterns within the brain and nervous system.

This is now the beginning of a new and empowering thought pattern, which will lead to a new and empowering attitude, thus forming new and empowering habits, and producing a new and empowering life.

Simple Lifestyle Adjustments:

<u>*Eight Hours*</u>

Many of the negative conditions spawned from sleep deprivation are often underestimated.

Some of these are fairly obvious such as drowsiness, fatigue, impaired concentration, mood swings and loss of short term memory; and then there are other effects which can be caused over time such as paranoia, shyness, withdrawal, immune deficiency, sickness, improper digestion and so forth.

As far as our sense of self-confidence is concerned; generally speaking, sleep deprivation can also cause us to make careless errors throughout our day-to-day communications and activities. This alone may potentially affect our self-confidence because as earlier stated; confidence can be intrinsically connected to competence.

If we are not competent toward a particular task—due to lethargy or an inability to focus—this can affect our self-confidence in that area. In order for our brain to function at an optimum level, it is generally recommended that we get at least seven hours sleep each night.

Yes, it's also true that some of us may naturally need more than seven hours; while conversely, some of us may need even less. Either way, it is worth due consideration. Gauge what works for you and then endeavour to stick with that.

The point here is to take adequate time to "recharge the batteries" each night and you will feel a noticeable improvement in your level of assertiveness. This will lead to increased competence and therefore, increased self-confidence.

Diet

Our diet can also affect our self-confidence in a number of ways. This is because certain foods can actually influence how we think and behave.

Serotonin, being a neurotransmitter, is thought to be a significant contributor to feelings of happiness and wellbeing. It is known as *the mood regulator*. And its production is essential for defeating depression, which naturally enhances self-confidence.

The release of this chemical from the brain can be promoted and regulated by certain foods that contain the B vitamins. These foods include fish; legumes, nuts, leafy green vegetables and many more.

It is also believed that vitamin B6 is the main catalyst for the conversion of the amino acid Tryptophan, into Serotonin, which in turn regulates our mood.

It stands to reason that if you are not in a good mood, or you are feeling disheartened or depressed about something, then your self-confidence to perform with surety will be affected. A healthy balance of the B Vitamins consumed within your diet can assist with this, among many other things.

"Put simply, foods affect moods."
#TOOSYY

It is also a well known fact that consistently skipping breakfast can begin to cause anxiety and fatigue. And if we are not feeling energetic or healthy, as our will to *participate* dwindles; that alone can undermine our self-confidence. Put simply: foods affect moods.

Write It Down

Keeping a journal of our progress in any area can definitely assist with building self confidence; because this enables us to read it back at a later date and commend ourselves for the measurable progress achieved throughout that period of time.

Oftentimes we may not realise just how far we've come in our personal development; keeping notes of the progress that we have made along the way definitely helps to bring it all in to focus at a later date. This can then be used to build more confidence and motivation to spur us on to the next level.

Writing down our key strengths—along with any progress we have made in dealing with any contrasting weaknesses—can be equally beneficial, as we've covered within the last chapter.

Something New

Learning something new is a sure-fire way to build self-confidence in our ability to take on the unexpected. This does not mean "try" something new (which implies just the once). It means *learn* something new (which implies a process); and keep going until you are competent in that area.

Learning a new skill raises our confidence for a number of reasons, for instance; when we overcome that initial stage of being totally incompetent (at a certain sport perhaps) and then we move on to the stage of "getting the hang of it," there is a certain feeling of surety that we gain as things begin to flow. This promotes self-confidence in our ability to adapt to a new task.

That same level of surety and confidence in our adaptive abilities can also be transferred into other areas of our lives and personality. We may then feel confident in taking on a new challenge elsewhere; put simply, we become more confident in our ability to "rise to the occasion."

A Compliment - From Me to Me

Complimenting yourself is not to be confused with being self-centred or arrogant, both of which are the spawn of an overactive ego. Instead, *complimenting yourself* is simply giving yourself a sincere pat on the back whenever you make notable progress; consequently refraining from *negative* self-criticism.

The worst kind of this disempowering criticism that we can endure is the kind that comes from ourselves. Stop putting yourself down or paying excessive attention to any flaws that you might have.

As we will explore later within *Mind your Mind;* our lives are governed by our most dominant thoughts. We manifest that which we focus on the most. So in this regard, over-focusing on the negative aspects will only bring more of those your way.

> **"When you talk yourself out of self-compliments, you rob yourself of a piece of self-confidence."**
>
> #TOOSYY

As we are on our journey of self development there may be times when we give in to temptation or make a few "mistakes." That's called: "being human." When this happens, we may want to criticise ourselves; but whenever we notice this pattern about to emerge, we can consciously interrupt it.

This can be done by simply remembering and focusing on some moments where you resisted temptation or made good progress. Perhaps this was even as simple as *not* buying the chocolate bar that you were about to buy; or perhaps you went out for that jog instead of talking yourself out of it.

Whatever the moments—remember them and then— compliment yourself for them. In fact compliment yourself for *any* progress that you have made. Don't just brush these achievements off; take a moment to acknowledge them. And the same would also apply with the compliments that you may receive from others.

Have you ever received a compliment such as "You look well today"? Of course you have! How did you respond? Did you do your best not to pay it any attention, or even try to brush it off with a reply like "Oh really, I think I look tired"? Or did you respond with a simple "Thank you"?

When you receive a genuine compliment, if you brush it off or reject it then you are indirectly telling yourself that you are unworthy of that compliment. Such thoughts will inevitably trigger the corresponding feelings of inferiority; thus lowering your self-confidence in the process.

The exact same principle applies with self-talk. Sometimes, when you talk yourself out of *self-compliments*, you rob yourself of a piece of *self-confidence*.

Exercise

Many of us may easily underestimate the importance of exercise when building self-confidence. And I am not solely referring to confidence derived from looking good. Admittedly there is some truth to the saying, "you feel as good as you look," however, exercising and being healthy will not only give you confidence based on appearance, but it will heighten your self-confidence overall.

You could start with a light exercise programme to begin with; and as you progress throughout that programme, naturally, you'll begin to accomplish more strenuous tasks; each time pushing yourself just that little bit further. This alone can boost self-confidence by providing a new sense of achievement, which will broaden out into other areas where physical exertion is necessary.

You will then begin to feel more confident in handling certain tasks outside of the training environment; this could even be something as mundane as confidently carrying one or two extra bags of shopping from the store. Remember, self-confidence can oftentimes be measured by self-competence.

Exercising also promotes the release of endorphins. Endorphins are chemical compounds that are released from the pituitary gland within the brain; they can calm the nerves and lower stress levels, thus promoting a greater sense of self-confidence.

Posture

Your mental attitude can also be influenced by your physical posture. If you walk around with your head held low, this may encourage feelings of low self-confidence. Likewise, if you are continually prone to slouch when sitting in a chair, this may encourage an attitude of laziness or indifference. When you begin to adopt a more assertive physical posture you will be amazed at the effect it has on your mental attitude.

It can be very easy to get into a slouchy type posture and mood if we have just been faced with the news of a setback; or something that we were counting on didn't go according to plan.

This can sometimes have a de-motivating influence on our overall level of enthusiasm, however, when you notice yourself in this type of mood, remember that you have the ability to influence how you feel by shifting your posture to a more assertive position.

Once you do this I guarantee that you will begin to feel more motivated, assertive, focused and therefore more *confident* to take on whatever the challenge may be (for more on this, see page 204 - *A Physical Shift*).

Goal Setting

Goal setting is extremely important when it comes to building self-confidence; however, merely goal setting alone will not make the grade.

As we covered in *"Goal Scoring,"* it is the execution and accomplishment of the goals that will boost self-confidence. It could even be as small as dry cleaning a suit that you can wear to the next business networking event, where you will give out some business cards to attract new clients, or joint ventures.

Use your willpower to push past any self-doubt and complete the task. Once you have done so, you will often think to yourself, "that was easy." The successful completion of that task will elicit more self-confidence which will be based on the consistent accomplishment of your goals, no matter how small; yes, even dry cleaning a suit.

Breathe

Whenever you are in a situation where you find yourself feeling stressed or fearful, it could simply be a matter of time before those feelings translate into a depleted level of self-confidence. A very simple remedy is just to take some deep breaths. Take a slow deep breath in for 3-to-5 seconds, hold it in equally as long, and slowly release it for 5-to-7 seconds.

Repeat this cycle 5 times and it will instantly increase the amount of oxygen reaching the brain. This will consequently help to counteract those feelings of stress, anxiety or fear, helping to regain a more relaxed, controlled and confident perspective toward the situation at hand.

<u>*Affirmations*</u>

Every day, tell yourself audibly—and with conviction—that you are confident in your abilities and it is only a matter of time before you imprint this message upon your subconscious mind.

You will then begin to naturally, and subtly, behave this way; often without even noticing it. We will continue to explore the benefits of using affirmations, in greater detail, within the chapter entitled: *Mind Your Mind.*

Now that our overall sense of *"self-worth"* has begun to promote our *"self-confidence"* we are truly *"becoming more"* from the inside, out. However, while peering from this wholesome inner vantage point, it's also imperative that we take a moment to address the number one inhibitor of man.

This is an emotion so widely misunderstood that it's been the single most common cause of unutilised potential throughout humanity. Yet on the other hand, when properly utilised and kept within reasonable limits, it could also be seen as one of the most influential driving forces available.

We will now learn of some concepts that may shift our outlook toward this emotion, and ultimately change our relationship with it to a much more empowering one. Nevertheless, before we can better-control or utilise this emotion, we must first better-comprehend it, so the question is…

Chapter 7

WHAT IS FEAR?

"Fears are educated into us, and can, if we wish, be educated out." – Karl Augustus Menninger

The word fear is a blanket term which is commonly used in two main contexts. In the first, it is used to describe a physiological response within the body, e.g., the feeling that you get internally, also referred to as, *the fight or flight response* (we will refer to this as "type 1").

And in the second main context, the word fear is typically used to describe our varying levels of imaginative worries, e.g., fear of rejection, fear of failure and so on (we will refer to this as "type 2"). Throughout the first part of this chapter, until the section headed *"Fear & Imagination,"* we will be addressing *type 1*.

The Misconception

It is a common misconception that courage is the complete absence of that which we call fear. In many cases, this is simply not true. Courage is the transmutation of fear but not the complete absence of it. When one develops courage the "fear" itself is still there, but it is just translated differently by the person experiencing it. Instead of a barrier that inhibits them, it's used as more of a driving force that propels them forward.

To further illustrate this point, some years back when I was fairly new to public speaking, I once asked a friend of mine— who at the time was a seasoned motivational speaker; "What's it like before you go up on stage to speak, do you still get nervous?" His reply was that he didn't get nervous, *he got excited*. "Excited?" I asked. He then replied, "Yes, just before I go on stage I love it, I get excited."

He described the feeling as a rush of energy in the pit of his stomach; he then went on to say that his hands begin to shake a little, and he also gets a tingly type of sensation throughout his body, he described this as "the rush." To finish off he then said; "when I get that rush of energy, I can take on anything."

The next day I asked an inexperienced speaker the same question: "What's it like before you go up on stage to speak, do you still get nervous?" His answer was that he gets extremely nervous just before going up to speak, even to the point where he almost doesn't want to follow through at all. He then said to me that his hands start shaking, he feels a "weird" energy in the pit of his stomach, and a tingly feeling throughout his body.

So what's the point? The point here is this: both of these men experienced the same feeling, but one of them chose to utilise it as a sense of excitement and power, and the other, a barrier and a weakness.

Now, of course there is the extreme end of the spectrum where a completely uncontrolled fear can literally paralyse the person experiencing it. In this case, due to a sudden and mass overdrive of hormones it can trigger mental and physical confusion; causing us to behave in a severely limited fashion by stifling our sense of logic and creativity.

But even this can be the result of how we are choosing to *label and interpret* that feeling. This is true on a conscious and subconscious level.

The word, better still; *the label,* "fear," is one that is commonly used in a disempowering and negative emotional context for obvious reasons. However, if we remove the label and just take an objective look at the energy itself; providing that it's kept within reasonable limits—it can in fact be utilised to our advantage; just as the experienced Motivational Speaker did when he chose to interpret it differently.

Fear as a label

Franklin D. Roosevelt once said, *"The only thing we have to fear is fear itself,"* but for the purpose of this chapter I would say, *"The only thing we have to fear is fear, misunderstood."* Without an adequate understanding of that which we label as "fear," we stand little chance of overcoming or utilising it, hence the saying; *"People fear what they don't understand."*

With a relatively simple shift in our perspective toward fear, we can also begin to free ourselves from being mentally held as prisoners of our own imagination.

The first thing for us to understand here is that; in many cases "fear" is simply a word that we use as a label. And it's a label for the feeling that we experience when certain hormones— adrenaline, cortisol and noradrenaline—are collectively released into the bloodstream. But as adrenaline is the chief hormone of the adrenal response known as "fight or flight," let's take a closer look at its role within this process.

Adrenaline

So, what exactly is adrenaline? Well, technically; adrenalin (also known as epinephrine) is a chemical which is released from minute glands that are located on top of the kidneys. These glands are triggered to release this hormone by commands to the sympathetic nervous system, from the part of the brain called the hypothalamus.

This happens once another part of the brain known as the Amygdala (which is specialised for reacting to stimuli and triggering a physiological response) sends this information to the cortex and hypothalamus. The command is then given to the adrenal glands to release adrenaline (along with cortisol and noradrenalin) into the bloodstream; and this is typically labelled as the *fight or flight response.*

We then experience that feeling (sometimes referred to as, butterflies) in the pit of our stomach, as blood is directed away from our digestive system and rushed into our muscles, anticipating action. This is a primitive and automated survival system, hardwired within fundamental human biochemistry through evolution.

The level of control that one has over this biological response is directly in line with the level of control they have over what their brain *subconsciously* perceives as a "threat," or at the very least "a challenge."

A quick surge of adrenaline into the bloodstream is the human body's way of preparing itself for immediate action. With that said; an obvious question here might be: If what we sometimes call fear is really just adrenaline, is fear a weakness or not?

I would say the word "fear" itself is the weakness. Adrenaline, kept within reasonable limits, can be utilised as a source of strength. However, many of us were never taught to consider this perspective when dealing with fear, therefore, to take this approach is generally not "the norm" within society.

So why exactly have I said that the word "fear" itself is the weakness? For a clearer understanding, let's take a quick look at how we process information on a basic level. First off; one of the primary ways that the human brain makes sense of what we experience is by association.

This is the basis of all human interpretation. The meanings that we assign to things become embedded neurologically and determine our outlook on reality.

The thing here is that, most of us have become so accustomed to associating the word "fear" with the state of "weakness," that the two meanings have generally become linked neurologically (fear = weakness = helplessness).

Simultaneously—due to conditioning—we then associate the fight or flight response with the word fear (adrenaline = fear = weakness = helplessness) and as a result, dependent on the context, the release of adrenaline—in terms of the fight or flight response—is then translated as "weakness."

For this reason, type 1 fear is commonly perceived as a weakness and an undesirable emotion, which many people are subconsciously ashamed to admit they have in certain areas.

We will take a look at a more empowering approach toward handling this type 1 fear a little later, but for now let's take a brief look at type 2 and how it affects our imagination?

Fear & Imagination

In the year 2008 a study was conducted as an attempt to determine how many of our type 2 (imaginative) fears actually happen to us. This study concluded that on average, ninety percent of these fears never occur. *Ninety percent!* Think of all that time and energy wasted contemplating the *"what if's:"* needlessly worrying about things that will never even happen to us.

This is where type 2 fear (worry, stress, negative imagination, etc.) can be particularly unhealthy because it stimulates type 1 fear (the fight or flight response)—sometimes unnecessarily, and begins to flood the body with adrenaline, cortisol and noradrenalin in preparation of a *real* threat, but it's all just imaginary.

Too many of these hormones released into the bloodstream unnecessarily, not only overdose the system, but also upset the balance of the body as they are specifically designed to deal with the *short term* and immediate stress, that could ensue from a situation of *real* danger.

"Ninety percent of our fears never happen to us."
#TOOSYY

Now, for sure, there are fears that may exist within the imagination that are based on factual evidence (get too close, and the fire *will* burn you); nonetheless, there are also fears *within* the imagination, based *entirely on* the imagination.

This is where there is no *real* threat, but only a *perceived* threat (fear of public speaking, fear of UK house spiders, and so on). Many of which have their roots in our tendency to fear the unknown; which again, in many cases, is due to a negatively programmed overactive imagination.

With this in mind I would venture as far as to say; not only do 90 percent of these fears never actually happen to us—according to the statistic—but at least 70 percent of those are based on lack of knowledge (the unknown) of that which we fear. And this lack of knowledge can then cause us to fill the gaps in our understanding, by using our imagination.

This can indeed be precarious because the conclusions that we arrive at, can then sometimes become a part of our very own belief system: u*nverified!* Of course, this process is entirely neutral; however, the issue with filing these "lack of knowledge gaps" with scenarios from our own imagination is that most of us are not usually optimistic enough in this area.

This can be due to our fair share of negative societal programming, which can sometimes cause us to imagine the worst case scenarios when pondering the unknown. We then compensate for our lack of knowledge in a particular area, with these imagined scenarios. And when this happens it is fertile ground for the cultivation of irrational fear, spawned by ignorance.

If we are not careful we can then become prisoners of those fears, possibly for an entire lifetime; or at least until we overcome them by studying, facing and understanding those things that we fear. After which we realise they wasn't so bad in the first place.

I'm sure you've probably heard the common acronym for F.E.A.R: False Evidence Appearing Real. It is this irrational imaginary-based type of fear that is most troublesome, because unlike a real situation that would come and go; type 2 fears exist completely within our minds.

Therefore they have the capacity to stay with us for much longer periods, and when allowed free reign of our imagination; they needlessly trigger our fight or flight response with continuous false alarms.

The reason for this is because the human nervous system (an extension of the brain) cannot tell the difference from an event that is actually happening, and an event that is happening purely within the imagination. What does this mean exactly? Good question! To shed some more light, let's look at the following illustrations.

The Experiments

The power of visualisation is studied within the field of *psychoneuromuscular activity*. Within a number of studies it has been proven time, and again, that an activity which is vividly imagined can produce electrical responses in the muscles and nerves, similar to those which are produced within the actual activity. In one of the most well known visualisation experiments (12) Russian scientists compared four groups of athletes who were training for the 1980 Olympic winter games. Each Group had a different training schedule:

Group One - 100% Physical Training

Group Two – 75% Physical training with 25% mental training.

Group Three – 50 % physical training and 50% mental training

Group Four – 75 % mental training and 25% physical training

In contrast to the results most of the world would have expected to see, Group four *with the majority of their time devoted to mental training* actually performed the best.

In yet another study, researchers at the Cleveland Clinic Foundation, Ohio, discovered that muscles can be strengthened just by thinking about exercising them (13). The experiment consisted of two groups of participants.

Group one, which had a team of thirty people, were asked to imagine using the muscle in their little finger, but without actually moving the finger itself. They were then asked to think as vividly as possible about moving this muscle and to make the imaginary movement as real as they could.

They did this for just five minutes a day, five days a week for a total of twelve weeks. After this period, they had their results compared to group two, who did no imaginary exercises throughout the same period of time.

The results revealed all. The participants in group one had actually increased the muscle strength in their little finger by 35 percent.

On top of this, brain scans taken after the study showed greater and more focused activity in the prefrontal cortex (the part of the brain dealing with, complex cognitive behaviour, personality expression and decision making) than before. The researchers concluded that the strength gains were due to the brains ability to signal muscle.

Lastly, to further demonstrate the fact that our imagination can affect us physically, we need only recall a bad (or pleasurable) dream. Without getting into a discussion on alternate realities— it would be logical to say that when we are dreaming, this is happening purely within our imagination. Nonetheless, our heart rate still rises, our pulse rate increases and we may even begin to sweat.

So, what exactly is the point here? The point is that if we are constantly occupied with imagining these irrational type 2 fears, we are causing the body to have a physical reaction by keeping us in an ever-ready state of fight or flight. And as stated earlier, this means that our adrenalin and cortisol production stays in a state of overdrive, which can lead to conditions such as anxiety, chronic stress, lethargy and many others.

While the adrenal response can have certain short term physiological benefits; constant long term production has the adverse affect, potentially causing us to become more edgy, emotionally unstable, paranoid, irrational and even over-defensive.

Our appetite is also likely to decrease which means we intake less nutrients, and this affects the immune system which relies upon those same nutrients to do its job efficiently. And all this can be caused by needless worries. *Stop worrying!*

"But how does one stop 'excessive worrying'?" you might ask. Well to begin with, we can utilise our willpower to direct our focus away from any disempowering and negative thoughts that may arise (see: *what am I thinking right now?* pages 200 - 203).

Essentially, it would also be wise to limit that which may trigger the imagination to ponder these fears in the first place.

Be mindful of negative stimuli, whether the result of constantly watching or listening to the News, or reading the Newspapers (war, debt, murder, etc.) watching certain soap-operas (adultery, lies, deceit, etc.) watching horror movies (blood, gore, sadism etc.) internal/external negative dialogue (doubts, criticisms, needless comparisons, etc.) or even just associating with strictly pessimistic people.

All of these influences can add toward keeping us in varying degrees of the fight or flight response *unnecessarily.* And this can cause us to interpret an irrational fear, as something substantiated and major. Take the fear of UK house spiders for instance.

Spiders

Within various surveys conducted throughout the UK, a number of people were asked what their top ten fears were. On average, spiders were ranked second. Now ask yourself this: in a country where, on average, 99 percent of the spiders are completely

harmless to humans; why would so many people have such
trepidation of them?

The answer is simple; because most people do not know (or at
least acknowledge) that "99 percent of the spiders are
completely harmless," and therefore their fear is more so of the
unknown—unsubstantiated and based on imagination. In
addition to this, it's an irrational fear that many of us have
simply adopted from others?

For instance, this fear could have been passed down from our
parents; who in turn had it passed down from *their* parents, so
on and so forth. We may have even developed this type 2
(imagination based) fear by watching certain movies which
promoted it, or maybe we adopted it from peers, colleagues or
others in society: perhaps even all of these factors combined.

One thing is for certain: in the UK, our fear of house spiders is
near enough completely irrational and commonly adopted
through social conditioning, rather than the threat of *actual*
danger.

If a spider goes near a small child, oftentimes that child will
have no fear of the spider; however, he/she may *learn* to fear
them later on in life. The real question here is, based on what?

We are all conditioned in some way, shape or form to fear
certain things. Sometimes that conditioning can be beneficial,
(i.e., you won't purposely put your hand in fire, for fear of being
burnt) and other times it could be completely unnecessary and
based on utter nonsense and ignorance.

If you are one of the many people (as I was until a few years ago) that has a fear of common house spiders, please stop for a few seconds and ask yourself the following:

1) What is my fear of spiders based upon?

2) Has a UK house spider ever harmed me or anyone else that I know within the UK?

3) Has it ever been common knowledge that house spiders in the UK are dangerous or poisonous?

4) Does the amount of legs an animal has determine how dangerous it is?

5) Does a spider have less of a "right to live," than I do?

If the fear of spiders applies to you directly; you may even wish to add a few questions of your own here; this is assuming that you are serious enough about overcoming this.

So many people state that they do not want to be afraid of certain things, but then they fail to take the necessary action to alleviate the fear, and therefore they remain prisoner to it: *Take action!*

Oftentimes, it may not even be the spider itself that you fear; but instead, what you fear, is the having to *overcome* that fear. Therefore it is completely internal and the power and ability to change it belongs to you, not the spider.

Once you have answered the foregoing 5 questions honestly within yourself, you may (or may not) be surprised at how soon you experience some degree of relief from your trepidation of these little creatures. A little research will also reveal that, not only are 99 percent of all house spiders within the UK completely harmless, but they can actually be a benefit to the household because they eat the bugs that *do bite* humans.

Of course; spiders were just used here as an example for the purpose of this exercise, you can analyse near enough any fear that you have in a similar fashion. The point here is; if you question anything enough you will begin to doubt it, and this is particularly the case with these unsubstantiated type 2 fears that reside within the imagination.

So, now that we've had a look at type 2 fears; how about if we are in a *real* situation where we experience the physical response of type 1 fear; can it then be used to our benefit in any way?

Short Term Benefits

Providing that our adrenal response is *justified* and not solely caused by an overactive imagination—there's a more empowering approach that one can adopt toward it.

Along with relabeling the adrenal response, as we covered earlier, the insights we're about to cover may also help to transform our relationship with type 1 fear, in order that we can then use it as a source of energy as opposed to a barrier.

First and foremost, if we find ourselves in a *real* situation where we are forced to act, adrenaline can actually be used to our benefit providing that it's kept within reasonable limits by the imagination being kept under control.

Here's the reason why; under acute stress, the body's sympathetic nervous system prepares us for short term vigorous action. As we covered earlier, when we are in a situation where we experience type 1 fear, we get a sudden influx of adrenaline (and other hormones) released into the bloodstream, which can cause us to become immediately physically stronger.

This is because the release of these hormones stimulates the nervous system to tap into reserves of energy that normally remain inaccessible.

According to Vladimir Zatsiorsky (14), a professor of kinesiology at Penn State University, USA, (who has extensively studied the biomechanics of weightlifting and is a well respected authority in this field, having trained hundreds of elite athletes) we as humans only use 65-to-80 percent of our "total muscle power" under normal conditions.

However, when we are faced with imminent danger, the body immediately prepares itself to utilise a higher percentage of our total muscle power, and this is what happens:

1) Blood rushes to the major organs making them stronger

2) Blood and oxygen rushes into our muscles making them stronger

3) Our pupils dilate for enhanced vision

4) Our overall sense of awareness is increased

5) We have less perception of pain

6) Airflow to the lungs increases

7) Our perception of time is slowed down

8) Our reflexes can become twice as fast

Now honestly, does this description sound like a weakness to you? Or does it sound like some rather advantageous abilities to have, even if only for a relatively short period of time?

If your answer was *yes* to the latter, then you are absolutely right, however, lack of understanding generally causes most of us to label this as a weakness, and therefore we act in accordance with this belief.

Nobel Prize winning Physicist, Max Planck, once said, *"When you change the way you look at things, the things you look at change."*

With this in mind, if we look at the adrenal response for what it is—a temporary source of physical power—then we will automatically be more empowered whenever we experience it, in a *real* situation. It will then take on a new meaning and, as we covered earlier, it's the meaning that we attribute to something which determines the type of action that we take toward (or away from) it.

Super Human Activity

Like many others, I once read the true story about a fairly young lady who singlehandedly lifted up a car with her bare hands, in order to rescue her friend who had been trapped underneath.

It would be fair to assume that, this lady would have been in a state of type 1 fear for her friend's life at that time. And as a result she unquestionably utilised the physical advantages of the same energy that causes others to feel helpless, because whether she noticed it at the time or not, she translated it differently.

Imagine all of the opportunities that have passed us by, based on that old disempowering relationship with fear. The good news is that we can change this relationship, and realise that it can be utilised as an advantage, rather than a weakness, in near enough any *real* situation where it is generated. This is providing that it is not given free reign over the imagination and allowed to spiral out of control.

To add to this, it is also a well known fact among zoologists that most wild animals will assail due to "fear," not courage. We too can assail near enough any of life's challenges, particularly once we begin to utilise this emotion—kept within reasonable limits—as a propellant rather than a hindrance. And this can be done by redefining our interpretation of the fight or flight response when and where necessary.

> "The meaning that we attribute to something, then determines how we feel about that thing."
>
> #TOOSYY

Now, does this mean that we should go about our day-to-day lives, wanting to elicit type 1 fear in order that we may become physically stronger? No, it doesn't mean that! Obviously, overall, the less stress of any type, the better.

The underlying purpose for the information within this chapter is that we may adopt a more empowering approach toward dealing with this emotion if it arises when justified: as opposed to becoming disempowered and therefore limited by it.

It is also important that after a short burst of adrenaline and cortisol (the fight or flight response) into the bloodstream, that we trigger the body's relaxation response in order that our bodily functions may return to a state of homeostasis (balance).

A glass of water along with 15 slow deep breaths is a simple, free and effective way to do this. This can also be beneficial for calming us down if we experience the adrenal response (type 1), triggered as a result of our imagination alone (type 2).

The Main Three

If you take nothing else from this chapter, let it be these three main points; of which the rest, pretty-much, subdivide into:

1) What we sometimes label as the feeling of fear, is really adrenaline, and adrenaline kept within reasonable limits is a performance enhancing hormone. And as such it can be a source of energy and excitement, rather than negativity and weakness.

2) The label that we give something is what determines what that thing means to us, and therefore how we feel about it. If we label *adrenaline* as "fear" we are more likely to be limited by it. Someone else could have the exact same feeling of adrenaline and label it as "excitement" or "power," and they would be far more likely to take action and get the result, where the first person wouldn't have.

3) Ninety percent of our fears never even happen to us. They reside purely in our imagination. And seventy percent of *those* are based on ignorance, so don't let the

imagination run wild with projected fears. Limiting exposure to any stimuli that may trigger this needless worrying is paramount. If we are constantly in a state of stress as the result of unsubstantiated fears, then this can cause an overdrive of the bodies fight or flight response, which can have negative side effects for the body and mind. Like any other performance enhancing substance, an "overdose" of adrenaline (or cortisol) can be detrimental.

A type of unsubstantiated fear can also manifest as "the-fear-of-change," and this can occur on the most basic of levels, such as not wanting to explore new things for instance; particularly if we have become overly accustomed to a set routine, and thus fearing the change of implementing something differently from time to time.

In this case breaking up that set routine a little can help to reintroduce us to a sense of variety. We then become less apprehensive toward displaying our true "*self worth*" when reaching out with "*confidence*" and doing something new without any need to ask the question: "*what is fear?*" Beyond any shadow of a doubt, we are now "*becoming more.*"

However, we will also become better equipped to traverse any barrier once we overcome the perceived "risk," of venturing into new and different territory. And to further accentuate our development within this area, in addition, we need to cultivate a healthy sense of…

WHAT IS FEAR?

Chapter 8

BALANCE

"We come into this world head first and go out feet first; in between it's all a matter of balance." – Paul Boese

Balance is a principle which is essential to life as we know it, on every level. It is such an important principle that it not only relates to human nature and perception, as many of the other topics throughout this book, but it is also perpetual throughout existence on the whole.

Firstly, I would like to take a moment to illustrate this on a grand scale—exploring how balance primarily influences all forms of life on earth—before relating its importance to human nature specifically; and why it is considered a quintessential aspect of *"Becoming More."*

Balance in Nature

Most of us are aware of the fact that H20 (water) is the pivotal ingredient for 99.9 percent of life and survival on earth. Of course, ice and steam are also both forms of water; however we need the correct *balance* between the two in order for life to flourish on this beautiful planet.

As we are dependent on this state of balance for water to exist within its liquid form, the water itself is moreover dependent on the principle of balance within the solar system, because it needs the right temperature to exist.

If this planet was considerably further away from the sun, then all the water here would be ice. And by contrast, if the planet was considerably closer to the sun, then the water would evaporate into a gaseous state. In both cases, life as we know it would not exist without the principle of *balance.*

Furthermore, this same principle of balance also applies to the Earth orbiting the Sun. Most conventional scientists will agree that the sun accounts for near enough 98 percent of all the mass within our solar system, and therefore has a very strong gravitational pull on the planets (within the solar system) many millions of miles away.

As one of those planets; Earth is travelling through space at roughly 67,000 miles per hour trying to escape this gravitational pull of the Sun.

As the Sun pulls the planets inward, the planets are trying to escape, pulling outward, and it is this *balance* between the two forces which creates an orbit. Without this we would not be revolving around the sun and life as we know it would cease to exist. And all of this is taking place as the planet *balances* on its axis.

OK. So that's on a bigger scale, but how about the microcosm (smaller scale)? Even there, the same applies. It's commonly accepted that atoms are the building blocks of the physical world: to put it simply; no atoms, no physical world. And just as our planet revolves around the sun, the electrons of an atom are believed to revolve around its nucleus, without which there would be no atom. This yet again is illustrative of the perpetual significance of balance.

Balance Well Acknowledged

Balance is also a principle very well acknowledged within the numerous forms of mathematics, philosophical teachings, religions, and sciences commonly practiced within many cultures worldwide: ancient through to modern. And its significance can be evidenced by the countless references and depictions throughout.

Whether it be the Scales of MAAT in ancient Egypt, the Tetrahedron used to this day in mathematics, the Ying/Yang Symbol commonly used in Chinese culture, the Merkabah in Judaism or even the Caduceus (kundalini symbol) used to this day within modern medicine; one thing appears certain: the principle of balance throughout existence is considered a foremost and essential one.

Furthermore, this principle of balance within our own lifestyle is just as important to us, as it is to our ability to walk or carry out any other physical activity for that matter.

"This principle of balance within our own lifestyle is just as important to us, as it is to our ability to walk."

#TOOSYY

Fuller Expression

Take a minute to consider this; the planet Earth is the living organism from which the human body has evolved, and we therefore intrinsically have many parallels with it: the microcosm generally reflecting the principles of the macrocosm, with the only differences being those of degree.

As we breath, as does the planet contract and expand. As we are subject to changes of mood, as is the planet; we call these seasons. Our Alpha Brain Waves (7.83 Hz) are an exact match to the planet's own natural energy field (Schumann resonance) 7.83 Hz. The human body consists of approximately 70 percent water, as does the planet also consist of 70 percent water, and the list goes on and on.

From this perspective of similarities, it would stand to reason that if the principle of balance is pivotal to the planet earth and therefore *its* nature, then the same would also apply with *human* nature.

"So, what's the point here?" you might ask. Good question! Well firstly; other than being dependent on varying degrees of balance, nature is also constantly seeking fuller expression of itself. We call this evolution.

And as an extension of *nature,* we are also intrinsically programmed to seek *fuller expression of our potential* (even though we don't always do this in the most beneficial ways). However, we achieve this best by maintaining a healthy sense of balance between what I call *The Three Major Areas.*

The Three Major Areas

The principle of balance is particularly important within the three major areas of our lives, being: our *mental, physical* and *spiritual* growth. The late, Wallace D. Wattles put it best in his book *The Science of Getting Rich* (15), when he said...

"No one of the three—body, mind, or soul—can live fully if either of the others is cut short of life and expression. It is not right or noble to live only for the soul and deny the mind or body; and it is wrong to live for the intellect and deny body or soul. We are also all acquainted with the loathsome consequences of living for the body and denying both mind and soul. Whatever he can say, no man can be really happy or satisfied unless his body is living fully in every function, and unless the same is true of his mind and his soul."

And to develop all three—thus maximising our *physical* health, *mental* capacity and *spiritual* potential—we must first cultivate more *balance* between them. Anyone who has experienced this knows it to be true.

When we are developing ourselves in all three of these major areas we naturally feel more fulfilled and life becomes more meaningful. Put simply, it's the opposite of *imbalance* within our lives, and we all know when there is an imbalance because we feel it somewhere deep within the centre of our being.

Imbalance

Imbalance of the scales could be caused by constantly disregarding our health for the pleasure of eating what merely tastes nice, overlooking our personal growth and development for the constant need to be entertained, abandoning our spiritual development for material gains, and the list goes on.

Of course we can work to develop these areas one at a time if need be, so long as we are careful not to over-focus on any one of them to the point that we severely neglect the others.

A balanced variety keeps us open-minded enough to notice opportunities where we may not have done otherwise.

#TOOSYY

"Variety is the spice of life that gives it all its flavour," said William Cowper. A *balanced* variety keeps us open-minded enough to notice opportunities where we may not have done otherwise. And the reason for this is due to our level of awareness.

When we become increasingly focused on the tedious habits of a droning routine, a typically biased mindset develops. And this not only limits our awareness but also the degree of balance within our own lives, consequently promoting narrow-mindedness.

If we are not exercising enough of our potential by broadening our capabilities and stretching the fabric of our intellect, it's likely that we begin to experience a lack of fulfilment within our lives.

Monotony can then subtly begin to suffocate both our *creativity* and *ambition*. When we feel particularly lacking in these two areas it can be a sure-fire sign that we need to implement more variety within our routines.

Now, say for instance that you are a parent who works a full time job; and upon returning home each evening imminently has to prepare "needs-must" for the children. You may be thinking at this point, "I don't have enough time to add more balance into my routine." But due to the mere fact that you are reading these words right now; I would say that you have already begun.

Furthermore, it may do you well to consider that adding more balance to your routine need not be a dramatic overhaul. You could quite easily begin with some relatively simple yet, often overlooked, effective changes.

Some of these might include: taking different routes to regular destinations, waking up at slightly different times a couple days a week, trying out some new foods and recipes, visiting some new and different types of places that you wouldn't usually go to, meeting new people and networking, balancing the free time spent in front of the television, reading more books like this while commuting to work or before retiring to bed.

Even things like learning two new words a day from a new language, listening to some new and different types of music, listening to some personal development audio programmes as an alternative to the radio in your vehicle, adopting some breathing exercises, meditating, joining the gym, going for a jog, or virtually anything that takes you out of your comfort zone, as *out of it,* is where we grow the most.

So break up the routine a little; wake up the routine a little; *shake* up the routine a little, and you will begin to feel more alive again.

Mediocrity

Many of us have the innate ability to perform some *exceptional* skills; however, because we have yet to attempt the things that would allow those skills to flourish, sometimes they go completely unnoticed—even for an entire lifetime.

Meanwhile, we might look at others who are successful in those areas through a subconscious veil of envy, thinking; "If only I could do what they do, then I too would be successful." Yet we fail to realise that if we had only just implemented a little more variety and tried out that thing in the first place, we too could have excelled within that field.

Instead, many of us chose to avoid the *perceived* risk of failure, and this need to "play it safe" by sticking to the *middle-line* often signifies the death of our dreams and ambitions, not to mention our creativity.

Just as the *rhythm of life* is signified on the ECG machine by many ups and downs, the same is also true within our own lives. However, due to our constant desire to avert some type of *perceived* risk and avoid the "downs" we also sacrifice the "ups" and, thereby, the rhythm of life itself.

As the Roman Emperor, Tacticus, once put it; "*The desire for safety stands against every great and noble enterprise.*" With this in mind, we must constantly resist the temptation of unnecessarily playing it safe with stale mediocrity.

The same could also be said of our willingness to seek refuge behind a veneer of excuses as to why we are not seeking fuller expression of our lives. *"I'm too this"* or *"I'm too that"* or *"I can't do this"* or *"I can't do that,"* are all commonplace variations of this willingness to accept tedium.

On the other hand, this does not mean that we run completely wild and off-the-rails, risking any-and-everything at a moment's notice.

It simply means that we take the necessary action to push through whatever excuses we have become accustomed to telling ourselves, and adopt more variety and balance into our lives, periodically stepping into the unknown and *out of the comfort zone.*

When we do this, we suddenly feel more alive within ourselves because we are naturally stimulating a wider range of our more-than-often dormant potential. *Whatever your excuse is; now is the time to stop believing it!*

We can remove the "mental blinkers" acquired as the result of monotonous routines, and begin to widen our range of perspective. Consequently, we then become more self-expressive and break free from the confines of self-made doubts and excuses. This can be initiated by making a definitive decision *right now* to take action in this regard.

You need not attempt to apply everything at once, by all means start small. As we saw back in the chapter on *Steadfast:* small changes can make huge differences over a period of time; because when applied with consistency, you then gain the great and powerful driving force of *momentum.*

Once we gather enough momentum, it becomes easier for us to achieve the same results at a later date with less effort; this is occasionally referred to as, *the snowball effect.*

Sometimes, the hardest part is starting, nonetheless the fact that you are reading these words is testament to the fact that you have already begun; *keep that momentum going.* Take action and add some more balance and variety, assuming that you haven't already.

Balancing the Routine:

Without a balanced variety within our routines, monotony takes charge and begins to stifle our creativity and self-motivation.

However, I would like to reiterate that adopting a more balanced attitude does not mean that we take on a "thousand things at once." It simply means that we vary the typical day-to-day droning routine with something different from time to time.

Constantly enduring the same monotonous routine can be anything other than mentally stimulating; thus our general outlook can begin to lack enthusiasm and as a result we feel less fulfilled.

Balance & Burnout

When committed to a certain routine, if we maintain some type of balance with our commitment, this alone can tend to lengthen the time that we stay committed. The *raison d'être* behind this— as contrary as it may sound— is; more balance, equals, less burnout.

Sometimes we can tend to experience a degree of burnout from committing to one routine too excessively, and thus *overindulging* in that particular area. Although this method of approach may *occasionally* be required where total immersion is absolutely necessary, there may also be times where this attitude may increase the chances that certain projects remain unfinished.

As far as the latter is concerned, here's the typical cycle: we have good intentions, start a project, overindulge, burn ourselves out, become bored, lose interest, and then we look for the next best thing. We have *more* good intentions, start *another* project, overindulge, burn ourselves out, become bored, lose interest, and then we look for the next best thing. We have *even* more good intentions, start yet another project … and on and on we go.

This can be counterproductive when aiming for lasting progress as it keeps us bouncing from extreme to extreme; as opposed to maintaining balance, interest and consistency throughout.

A good example of this may be well known by some of us that may have experienced "burnout," due to being overcommitted to seeing results while attending the gym.

Burnout at the Gym

At first we might start our new found regime with unrivalled enthusiasm and vigour, eager to excel in fitness, our every other thought or conversation revolving around our new hobby. We feel it is our duty to endure excessive two hour workouts until we can literally do no more. Of course pushing ourselves as far as possible is due to the anticipation of seeing noticeable gain in muscle, or loss of weight, *quickly.*

After a while, though, especially if not balanced with adequate rest and nutrition; this can cause physical and mental fatigue. Then we begin to slowly decline in our attendance eventually "putting-it-off" day by day, until we stop going all together.

However, had we just limited each of our gym sessions down to half, or even a quarter of the duration; this could have given us more to look forward to the next time, thus maintaining our interest over a longer period. As a result there would have been far less chance of us burning out and losing interest, after just a short period of time.

For another sporting example; you will very rarely see a professional boxer in the ring, against a worthy opponent, come out and give everything they've got *non-stop.* The boxer, if they have been trained well, may get off to an enthusiastic start but will still pace themselves accordingly in order to preserve their energy.

Likewise, if we maintain a consistent but steady pace throughout a process, chances are that we will preserve our enthusiasm, energy, interest, and therefore our level of determination for considerably longer.

This is especially true if it's a process that will take some time, as near enough anything does that we wish to master. In which case, it's best that we pace ourselves throughout.

If we constantly overindulge to overachieve, we risk burnout before completion of the process and by contrast, if we underachieve then we won't attain the desired results. Therefore, not over, not under, but *achieving* is key. Balance!

Now that we've taken a quick look at how variety and balance can benefit routine, can this same approach also be applied to a simple task? If need be, *yes it can.*

Balance On Task:

Whether you're a student with an important essay to write, an employee or employer with a vital document to draft, a musician with a song to compose, or a speaker with a speech to practice; there has probably been some time or another when you've had to deal with every creative person's nightmare: *The mental block.*

<u>The Mental Block</u>

We have probably all experienced a mental block at some point. It's usually that point where it seems like you have no new ideas flowing, and it has become increasingly challenging to "think outside the box." So, let's take a quick look at what actually causes a mental block?

As we covered earlier, subjecting ourselves to the same droning routine without any variety tends to dampen our ability to think outside the box. A mental block in one area could also be the result of our ongoing preoccupations in another, distracting our attention from the task at hand. Or perhaps, it could even be due to *trying too hard*, mentally racing straight past the obvious ideas. And of course, it could even be all of these factors combined.

But more than often, particularly when we are working toward a deadline, if we experience a mental block, it's because we are "standing too close to the picture."

We may need to "take a step back" in order for us to gain a better view of the whole situation. By doing this we are broadening our perspective and will thus be more likely to regain a more open-minded approach. This refreshes our perspective and allows more room for our creativity to flourish.

When we are sucked into the whirlwind of over-thinking, it only makes it more challenging for us to think creatively. Instead of putting yourself under even more pressure to meet the deadline, immediately stop what you are doing regardless of the time limit and focus on something else for a short while: break the pattern.

This should be something that will turn your attention away from the task at hand. As cliché as it sounds, you could go for a quick walk outside and really take a minute to notice the scenery, or you could simply take a moment to "think big."

Thinking Big

Momentarily *thinking big* will assist you with putting your task, back into perspective. Take a short break from the task at hand and think of something that inspires a sense of awe; that is to say, an almost overwhelming level of admiration.

If you have ever stood on a beach and looked out at nothing but the sea, can you remember how *vast* the view was?

Or consider how small this planet is in relation to the sun (it is said that almost 1.3 million Earths could fit inside the volume of

The Sun). Then consider that our Sun is just one of the smallest stars out of roughly 200 Billion within our galaxy alone. The intention here is not to get carried away with this train of thought, but to just briefly admire the immensity of the macrocosm (bigger picture).

"How random," you might be thinking. And you'd be right. It's completely unrelated to your task, and that's the whole point. But when you turn your attention back to the task at hand it should seem relatively small in comparison, and not so daunting. New ideas should begin to flow. You have overcome the mental block.

Perspective

Whatever your task, bringing it back into perspective can be achieved by regaining a state of open-mindedness. Sometimes this may require a degree of dissociation. If stuck for ideas, you could also ask yourself; "If I were watching a movie, how would I say the character in that movie should complete this task?"

This is a form of dissociation that can also help you to look at the picture from an "outside of the box mentality." After a short while many creative solutions may begin to flow from this perspective and when they do, don't spend too much time pondering if they are right or not, just get started and write them down, you can amend them later.

You will realise that after, perhaps, five minutes or so of writing down whatever comes to mind your creative ideas will gather momentum. Write down as many of these ideas as possible. Take a short break, maybe repeating the same process as before, and you will find that you have an even fresher perspective toward the task; instigating a renewed sense of creativity through a range of inspiring ideas.

Some of the ideas that spring to mind may be seemingly obvious, but nonetheless they are ideas that you didn't grasp while looking at the task for too long a time, without refreshing your perspective. Another method of approach that could assist in this area (and many more) is referred to as the Hakalau.

The Hakalau

The Hakalau (also known as *Peripheral Vision)* is a state of expanded awareness. It is very effective for inducing a state of heightened awareness and presence.

It is also a very powerful *creative* state to be in, especially when experiencing difficulties toward *thinking outside the box.* And the reason for this is because the Hakalau immediately broadens our perspective.

In day-to-day life it can be quite common for us to walk around with our "blinkers" on: restricted to viewing things through a type of tunnel-vision. From this narrow viewpoint things can sometimes seem a lot bigger, or worse, than they actually are, and thus out of proportion with reality itself.

As you read this right now, take both of your hands and place them at either side of your face by the corners of your eyes, do this so your hands are totally blocking your peripheral vision.

Notice that this book now seems a lot more prominent, or even slightly bigger than it actually is, when the peripheral view is blocked. Now remove your hands, become aware of your peripheral vision and observe the difference.

We need not use our hands to limit our peripheral vision to make things seem bigger, or harder, or worse, more complicated, or more prominent than they actually are. Many of us do this each day, mentally, by having tunnel-vision-focus toward our worries, our doubts, our habits, our deadlines and so on.

As a light example, picture this: you are in the process of giving up chocolate, and have told yourself that today will be the day. However, you've been out of the house for most of the day and when you return home, right there on your kitchen worktop is your favourite chocolate bar staring you in the face: bought for you by someone in the household who was none-the-wiser to your decision.

Now, all of a sudden—particularly if you have low willpower— that small bar of chocolate becomes a compelling and powerful temptation.

It has taken on a whole new life of its own within your imagination, and the reason for this is because; at that point there's a good chance that your awareness is now in "tunnel-vision-mode." You have become so focused on the, *should I, or shouldn't I, eat the chocolate?*" that all else virtually becomes momentarily invisible.

However, if willpower is not enough, by simply entertaining the Hakalau and expanding your awareness at that moment, no longer will your attention be solely focused on the chocolate bar because your perspective will be immediately broadened: put simply, you'll mentally take those blinkers off. The chocolate bar will then cease to be the dominating factor of your awareness. And of course this could apply with anything and not just chocolate.

So how do we enter into this state of Hakalau?

1. Pick a spot on the wall to look at, preferably just above eye level.

2. Focus all of your attention on that spot.

3. Allow your vision to begin spreading slowly outward from that spot, until you begin to notice the things that are in your peripheral vision.

4. Allow your peripheral vision to extend up to the ceiling both sides, and down to the floor both sides. Your awareness and focus has now expanded.

5. Now let's go one step further and expand your awareness to what's behind you, but without physically turning around. And do this while still maintaining the awareness of your peripheral vision. You are now simultaneously aware of everything that is around you. Your level of awareness has now expanded 360 degrees; your focus is on, no *one* thing

6. Notice all of the sounds that are present, near and far. It's likely that you begin to feel calm and relaxed whilst in this state. You will also sense a heightened state of presence.

In this state of mind there is no room for trivial thoughts and worries, and if they do arise, they have no emotional "pulling-power."

This means that they are not as major as they might have seemed while our attention was focusing on them disproportionately—with the "mental blinkers" blocking our peripheral awareness. This exercise is not to be underestimated. It is very simple to do, yet, when done correctly, it can be highly effective.

The Hakalau can also be very effective when it comes to *learning*.

This is because whilst in this state we are not only expanding our awareness, but we are also loosening our conscious barriers. Therefore we can take more in, allowing information to flow directly into the subconscious mind.

If you are someone who tends to adopt more of an *analytical* approach toward things, of course, being analytical is a great trait to have when paying attention to detail. However, it can also sometimes be the cause of us *over*-analysing things. When utilising the Hakalau, the analytical nature of the conscious mind is slightly more relaxed and thus information flows more easily into our subconscious mind, readily stored for recall at a later date.

This can be useful when we want to effectively retain information that we are learning (memorising information for a test, an exam or a speech perhaps) and allow the intake of such to flow, without us being too analytical or over-thinking the point. We will cover more on this within: *Mind your Mind.*

Balancing Your Nature:

Now that we have addressed the importance of utilising more
variety and balance within our daily routines, along with how to
implement *balance on task* and alleviate the mental block, how
about balancing one's own nature?

Lighten Up

For instance, if you are someone that tends to take them self,
and life, over-seriously; then it may help if you set a little time
aside each day for some "me-time." And use this to just simply
relax.

You could also use some of this time to do some things that
make you laugh and let go of this constant need to take yourself
so seriously. As simple and obvious as this sounds; it's amazing
how many of us get so caught up with current events that we
completely overlook or underestimate the simple things in life.

So go on, put your ego aside and call your inner child out to
play. It doesn't' mean that you go over board and become a
constant clown, but just bring some balance back to the scales. If
you have fairly young children then play with them and do some
things that make you laugh; things that your "over-serious and
self critical side," may normally consider childish or foolish.

As children we were far less self critical of our behaviour and
far more self-expressive. Yes, of course, as adults we have more
responsibilities but still, this does not mean that we must be
overly-serious, nor does it mean that we bear the burdens of the
world upon our shoulders. *Loosen up!*

By contrast, the same principle can also apply vice versa; if you are someone that is constantly jovial and care-free then you could take some time now-and-again to adopt a more serious perspective toward your goals; objectively analysing where you are right now in terms of your progress toward them, etc.

Needless to say, this will promote a more balanced outlook: one where you are in control of the *pendulum swing effect,* and not contrariwise.

The Pendulum Swing

The pendulum swing effect is most evident with those of us who tend to go from one extreme to another: the *all or nothing* attitude. Although this can be extremely productive when used in a positive context, outside of this it can lead to intemperance.

This determined *"I've started so I'll finish"* attitude is undeniably an essential quality to have in certain areas, but it can be equally as detrimental in others. And the pattern shows up in the small things right through to the major.

For example: instead of one or two biscuits we have a duty to finish the whole pack in one sitting, not just one slice of cake but the whole cake, not just one glass of wine but, "might as well finish the whole bottle," not just spending *some* of the money, but spending all of it. Intemperance has become habitual.

Before long we then reach a point of *sudden abstinence,* in hopes of reversing the tables; but more than likely after a period of time the cycle only tends to repeat itself. And like the pendulum, we swing back and forth from one extreme to the other.

When something has become almost habitual and we *suddenly and abruptly* cut it off; there may be a heightened chance that we will re-indulge twice as much at a later date.

The reason for this is that the harder you "swing the pendulum" in one direction, naturally the harder it will come back. Sudden abstinence then, at a later date, becomes sudden indulgence and there we go again, from extreme to extreme.

Generally, the majority of people—particularly those slightly deficient of willpower—will find that *weaning* themselves away (bit by bit) from a habit benefits them a lot more long-term. And this is because they are then less prone to fall victim to the sudden indulgence vs. sudden abstinence, tennis match.

Weaning away from unwanted habitual behaviour can reduce the chances of a person bouncing back and forth, from extreme to extreme; and in this regard it helps to reinstate a sense of balance within their nature, and therefore their life.

This weaning method can also strengthen our level of discipline and willpower to remain in control of the process, consecutively heightening self confidence.

The importance of weaning off of old habits is also demonstrated by the common use of nicotine patches (and the like) for smokers. The patches gradually decrease the dose of nicotine supplied to the wearer, in order to decrease the chances of stronger cravings caused by sudden abstinence.

Imagine flicking a rubber band: of course the further you pull it back and let go the further it will shoot. More tension one way equals more force the other. But if you were to pull back and then slowly control the tension as you were releasing it, then of course this would lessen the power of the shot.

In a similar way, slowly releasing a habit will also lessen the power of any future temptation toward it.

On a grand scale, as far as our lives are concerned, the importance of having some level of control over the pendulum swing effect is paramount. Without it we become *intemperately* prone to bouncing back and forth, from extreme to extreme: but with it we develop a greater degree of *balance* and self-control.

This concludes *the second cornerstone of potential* where we have begun to heighten our *self-worth* and *confidence;* while transforming our relationship with *fear* to a more *balanced* outlook.

We are now truly upon the path toward *becoming more* within ourselves. Let's now enter into the third cornerstone of potential and begin *utilising more.*

The End of Part Two

THE THIRD CORNERSTONE OF POTENTIAL

Utilising More

Chapter 9

SELF AWARENESS

"Everyone thinks of changing the world, but no one thinks of changing himself." – Leo Tolstoy

A friend of mine, Greg, once told me a story of what he called; "a weird one." He said that on the previous day, when he woke up, he was about to have a shower but found himself with no hot water because his gas supply had run out.

He had forgotten to credit his Prepay gas meter card the day before, so he rushed out to his local supermarket to top it up. When he walked into the store, Greg noticed that there were two people already being served by the cashier but otherwise, there was nobody else queuing. He then went and stood ("first in the queue") next in line to be served.

A few seconds later a couple more people came and stood behind him in the queue, but at this point Greg realised that he had also forgotten to buy bottled water.

So that he wouldn't lose his place in the queue, he told the lady behind him that he was coming back, and then quickly ran to the nearby fridge to get one.

When he came back to the checkout, a few seconds later, Greg saw that his place had apparently been taken by another man who was now stood in front of this lady, first in line.

Assuming this man had "pushed in," Greg then approached him and calmly suggested that he should go and take his rightful place at the back of the queue. Adamantly, the man replied that *he* had been first in the queue; standing there the whole time. He shook his head in disbelief at the audacity of Greg, and then appeared to look over at the cashier for support; the cashier timidly nodded in agreement with him.

Greg, still slightly confused, decided to compromise. Furthermore, if this man seriously thought that he had been first in the queue the whole time; perhaps he was "mentally challenged." So rather than escalate the situation any further, Greg let him go first and then he went next.

On his way back home, Greg began to replay the scenario in his mind. For a brief moment he thought: "what if the man in the queue *was* actually in the right?" Then Greg began to wonder if he was missing something. After all, that man was *so* certain that he was first in line; had he really been standing there the whole time?

As he replayed the memory over and over, Greg began to vaguely remember that as he walked into the shop initially, and glanced over at the checkout, other than the two people that were already being served, there *was indeed* someone else standing at the front of the queue.

And as the memory became clearer, this person happened to have on the same colour jacket as the man that Greg had just been telling to go to the back of the queue. This was simply because, *it was that man.*

He had been standing there, first in line, the whole time waiting patiently and minding his own business; then out of nowhere along came Greg telling him to "take his rightful place at the back of the queue." Never mind Greg thinking the man was "mentally challenged;" I'm sure that the man certainly thought similar, if not more unpleasant, thoughts about Greg.

So, how could something have been so obvious—as in, a whole person standing right there centimetres in front of Greg—and yet still go completely unnoticed? In short, the answer is one word: *Awareness.* At that moment, being preoccupied with having no hot water at home, Greg's awareness was focused elsewhere. And speaking of awareness, this reminds me of the story of the wealthy Persian farmer: Ali Hafed.

Ali Hafed, sold his farm to go out into the world in search of diamonds, but nonetheless he died poor and unsuccessful. Lo and behold, the person who bought the farm then discovered acres of diamonds, buried right there beneath the soil. Had Ali's awareness been focused on what was literally "underneath his nose," instead of hastily seeking treasures elsewhere, he wouldn't have died poor and unsuccessful with his endeavour.

Considering both of these stories; how many of us—just like Greg and Ali Hafed—are overlooking what's in plain sight? How many of us remain oblivious of what is "right underneath our noses" or "right in front of us"? And more importantly, why is this? Well, again, it's primarily because our awareness is focused elsewhere.

So if we take this same principle and apply it to *self* awareness, one could argue that we have a number of potential treasures within our own character (dormant skill-sets, character traits, qualities, etc.) that we are also overlooking; especially if our awareness is constantly focused *externally* (on the outside world), and not within self.

Although a predominately "introverted" person may tend to be more familiar with this notion than their "extroverted" counterparts, this does not negate the importance of this principle overall. Self-awareness is not merely having an introverted perspective, but also includes active self development in its entirety.

Does this mean that we should all become totally introverted? No, it doesn't mean that. It merely means that periodically turning our awareness inward is crucial for true self-development to occur. But as we saw throughout the last chapter, *balance is essential*.

Beneath The Surface

In the fast-paced modern society of today, many of us have increasingly busy lifestyles. This is true whether we are devoting the majority of our time and effort towards our careers, raising children, maintaining our households or in most cases, all three, and more.

With *"work hard, play hard"* being a familiar motto many of us have a desire to be entertained. And since there are so many new and exciting forms of technology, convenience gadgets and other stimuli that *keep* us stimulated and occupied, our thirst for external entertainment is quenched relatively easy.

But if this work-hard-play-hard pattern continues over a period of time, our self-awareness may begin to decline. And this is because our attention is being so continuously focused on external pleasures, that we hardly ever turn that same attention inward. Consequently some our potential remains unutilised; shrouded beneath our surface identity.

Self-awareness is having a clear, thorough—and sometimes objective—understanding of who you are as a person inclusive of your strengths, weaknesses, beliefs, values, morals, habits, thought patterns, emotional patterns, behavioural patterns and so on.

"But I already know who I am," you might say; and of course this is true to a degree. I mean sure; of course you know a few of your likes and dislikes or you might describe yourself as either outgoing or shy, flamboyant or reserved, rude or polite, fun or boring, or by various other adjectives.

However, many of these are in fact merely traits of our social masks. They can be seen as *effects* that manifest through our personality dependent on the situation. Conversely, self-awareness is the identification and management of the *cause* which is behind those effects.

For instance, have you ever behaved in a certain way and then regretted it later? When this happened you might have asked yourself after the event, "Why did I react in that way?" or "Why did I say that?" or "Why do I always get this feeling in that situation?" Or even, "Why do I have this phobia or that fear?" so on and so forth.

These are the types of questions that arise when we are seeking the *cause* of the effect. Although sometimes we may all need a little guidance to find them, our answers to these questions always reside internally.

They can be found through various simple exercises that strengthen our level of self-awareness and emotional intelligence (many of which can be found throughout this book).

We then begin to utilise, and identify with, a more profound and deeper-rooted powerful version of ourselves. Thus we begin to penetrate through the outer layers of the comparatively basic surface model, which is loosely referred to as: The Personality.

Personality

The word *Personality* originates from the Latin word *Persona*. The word "persona" in Latin, literally translates as: "*Mask.*"

Looking at these origins of the word *personality;* we could also liken what we refer to as such, to a type of "*social mask.*" But nonetheless, it's a social mask that we grow to accept as very real and substantial over the years. So how does this happen? Well, let's take a look at the basic process.

At some point within our lives the vast majority of us have had, do have, or will have, a desire for *more* of something. This is true whether that "something" is more respect, more significance, more love, more money, more time, more freedom, more courage, more friends, more recognition, more this, more that, and so on.

Consequently, we learn how to tailor our behaviour in accordance with that which will produce "more" of these things within our lives, in order to fill this perceived void.

This adaptation process usually begins at a fairly young age. And subtly, as the years go by, this way of behaving becomes like the "mask" that solidifies.

We then cultivate a personal narrative to validate this mask (personality). To put it simply; we develop a story that we tell ourselves, and others, in an attempt to justify why we are the way we are. (e.g.; "I have been through XYZ and it has made me *this* person," etc.)

We naturally begin to filter all new experiences through the boundaries of that narrative to further validate it, and we do this to the point of complete identification with it. (e.g.; "I am this way, it's all I can be, and that's just the way it is.")

This, in turn, shapes our social identity as people begin to interact with us in ways akin to how they expect us to respond, based on that narrative.

So, the narrative backs up the social mask; and we then have the tendency to define ourselves by the set qualities of that "mask" *(personality)*.

And it is this rigid definition that we adopt of ourselves which forms the parameters of the fortress, keeping us trapped within that *one* way of being.

Our scope of vision becomes limited by those parameters, but since these limitations are *self imposed* they can be redefined once we begin to regain a larger vision of ourselves.

As Einstein once said: *"You cannot solve a problem with the same type of thinking that created it"*, and similarly "you cannot see the whole picture when you are inside the frame."

This is why having a clear understanding of these distinctions is essential, as they can provide a vehicle for us to momentarily step outside of our predefined parameters and look at ourselves from a much wider perspective.

However; since your vision of yourself is naturally determined by your *point* of view at any *one* time; in essence, no matter who you think you are, you are *always* more than that.

I'm sure that at this point it's becoming clear that there is much more to you, than what is typically referred to as "your personality." Do not become so incessantly identified with the limited attributes of this "social mask" (outgoing or shy, flamboyant or reserved, rude or polite, fun or boring) that you fail to explore new possibilities of being.

> "The limitations that we accept are the limitations that we expect."
>
> #TOOSYY

Your social mask (personality) is not who you are in entirety. All possibilities exist within you at all times. And you can venture far beyond any self imposed limitations by first acknowledging this.

In many cases, we will not excel beyond our own opinion of ourselves; therefore the limitations that we accept are the limitations that we expect, and this then creates the paradigm through which we view life.

A healthy level of self-awareness, then, not only helps us to distinguish this; but also to positively influence the process to our liking, regardless of the labels that we identify with.

Mislabelling

Our personalities can also be influenced over the years by the opinions of others. For instance, if we were consistently complimented since childhood for a certain type of behaviour, then as we grow older we could easily start to become more confident in that area; which, of course, is fairly straightforward.

However, if we were constantly criticised for the exact same type of behaviour, we may have begun to experience feelings of inadequacy rather than confidence. Subsequently we may have labelled that same trait as undesirable and therefore as a weakness, rather than a strength.

The objective reality in both of these scenarios is that these compliments or criticisms are external and derived from the *opinions* of others. This does not change the fact that once they have been internalised over time, they can influence how we view ourselves.

If we are mislabelling some of our strengths as weaknesses or vice versa and actively discouraging certain elements of our character, this can become a serious hindrance to us becoming one with our true purpose. These factors are why a healthy level of self-awareness is so essential.

A healthy level of self-awareness also allows us to become more at one with ourselves, and thus we gain a greater level of control over our thought processes, along with our emotional reactions to persons, places or things.

Many—if not all—of the exercises, techniques, strategies and approaches found throughout this book will enhance self-awareness, simply because this book is one on *Self* Development. Nevertheless, we will now take a look at a few more simple exercises that will help to promote a heightened sense of self-awareness and emotional intelligence.

You may have already seen some of these covered elsewhere throughout this book, however, they have been repeated here for the benefit of your subconscious mind. Without further ado, the first of these simple exercises is to:

___Document it!___

This can sometimes be an essential element toward gaining self-awareness. Whether it's writing down our strengths and weaknesses, documenting some of our thoughts and feelings or even just recording any progress that we have made, to date; *documenting it* can serve as a powerful point of reference for gauging our development at a later date.

As the saying goes, "*If your life is worth living, then it's worth recording.*" Writing things down can also help to give us a clearer and more objective viewpoint within the corresponding areas.

When documenting our character strengths—now that we have been through the chapter on *self-worth,* and are less likely to be carried away with self-criticism—it is also equally important that we honestly identify any obvious "weaknesses."

Weaknesses are simply areas that need development. No matter how small, they can be viewed as material for a powerful reversal because in facing and overcoming them, there is much strength and, more importantly, *self-knowledge* to be gained.

In essence, the inscription on the Ancient Greek Temple of Apollo, at Delphi, left no room for misunderstanding: *"Know thyself and thou shalt know all the mysteries of the gods and the universe."*

Mirror-Talk

Following on from developing character strengths, there is another simple exercise that I like to call *Mirror Talk.* Certain comedians and actors might practice this exercise when first starting out; in order to strengthen the congruency between their facial expressions, body language, and their message. By doing so they become more aware of how they are portraying their demeanour at any given moment.

For instance, if you are someone that naturally wears a frown; the majority of the time you may not even notice when you're doing it. You could be talking to someone about something commonplace, and unknowingly be wearing a deep frown.

Due to this you could be misinterpreted, simply because your facial expression was incongruent with your message. Conversely, the same could be said of someone that naturally has a slight smirk; even when they are conveying a serious message.

For another example of this, look at some public speakers as they speak. You will notice that while some of them come across as rather genuine; others may come across as not so genuine. For the latter, you may also notice that their facial expressions, or their body language, are in some way incongruent with their message.

As a result they may seem equivocal, ungenuine, or at best, inexperienced. And yet, for the most part, this is simply because they are not self-aware of how dissonant their mannerisms are from their message.

So, now let's go ahead and see where you fit in on the scale of congruence. Take a minute to talk to yourself in the mirror; you can even imagine that you are talking to someone else. Banish the old saying that "Talking to yourself is the first sign of madness," if this were true then you would never think, let alone think allowed.

Now back to the point; talk to yourself in the mirror, or imagine that someone has asked you a question and you are simply responding to that person.

As you do this, notice if your facial expressions and body language are harmonizing with what you are saying? Also pay attention to your eyes, how are they moving? Can you look yourself in the eye while you talk, or do you feel the constant need to look away? How are your hands moving? Are you even using your hands?

Would an onlooker know what emotions you were attempting to convey if they couldn't hear you? In short, would you resemble the shifty leader, or the charismatic and genuine one?

With regular practice this exercise can help us to become more self-aware of our demeanour and how congruently we come across to others. We can then begin to utilise a wider range of expressions and this, in turn, will allow us to expand upon our range of behaviour.

Admittedly at first glance this exercise might seem a little quirky or foolish, but realise this: the reason that it may seem so is chiefly due to an indoctrinated element of societal conditioning that scoffs at the unconventional. It is this same conditioning that reinforces one's desire to conform to the "social norm" that we spoke about earlier.

In this light, such a simple exercise can also begin to release us from the confines of conventionalism. And along with strengthening our self-awareness it can also assist in overcoming excessive self-consciousness, which is usually due to wondering how we are appearing to others. We need not wonder if we already know.

"But isn't self-consciousness the same as being self-aware?" As far as the contexts in which they are typically used; no, they are not the same. There is a distinction to be made.

Self-consciousness is typically used in the context of being *excessively* conscious of one's appearance or manner, to the point of shyness or embarrassment, which can sometimes cause low self-esteem or paranoia.

With *excessive* self-consciousness we are consistently and *primarily* viewing ourselves from the outside, in. This means that we are continually prone to seeing ourselves through the lenses of others and their judgements of us. Some Psychologists refer to this as Public Self-consciousness (16).

However, with a healthy level of self-awareness we are viewing ourselves primarily from the inside, out. And moreover, we do so without the *excessive* need to introspect solely based on the fleeting opinions and judgements of others. And as a result of this we can also gain more emotional stability.

What am I Thinking Right Now?

It is a well known fact that, if repeated often enough, certain emotional states can become addictive and therefore habitual. This is as true of the positive states, as it is the negative. But needless to say the negative states can become more destructive, especially when they are "running on autopilot."

For instance, if you habitually become frustrated by relatively minor things; there may be times when—even though nothing per se has happened—you still find yourself feeling frustrated, without even knowing the reason why.

This could be because frustration has now become a habitual emotional pattern. Put simply; frustration feels like home, emotionally.

The paradox here is that; there are those of us who do not feel happy (satisfied) unless we're angry (frustrated). So we're constantly looking for reasons, and guess what? There is no shortage of them. We find them easily, not necessarily because the world is a bad place, but because people see the world as *they* are.

Although frustration has been used as the example here, this can also apply to many of the other negative emotional patterns that have become habitual through (sometimes unconscious) repetition.

Once we have become more self-aware, we automatically gain a greater level of control over these patterns. However; to disrupt and replace them, we must first recognise and catch them in action. Here's a good place to start. Randomly ask yourself this question at any given point throughout the day: *What am I thinking right now?*

"Is that it: 'what am I thinking right now'?" you ask. Yes, to begin with it's really that simple. By randomly asking ourselves this simple question we momentarily cease to be so "wrapped up" in our thoughts. Thus we step into the role of *observer;* objectively observing our thoughts or emotions.

This can make all the difference. "Why?" *because you cannot see the whole picture when you are inside of the frame.* By momentarily stepping outside of the "frame" of our thoughts, and thus becoming less identified with the "ramblings of the mind," a deeper level of self-awareness is gained.

When you ask yourself the question, "what am I thinking right now?" you may even be surprised at what you catch yourself thinking and how completely unnecessary or disempowering it might be.

Interrupting and replacing these negative thought patterns before they spiral out of control and become furthermore habitual, is an essential aspect of personal growth.

The next question is equally important, and that is; *why do I feel like this*? You may be surprised that sometimes you have no answer; or you may be surprised at how unrelated your answer (excuse) is to the present situation.

The key here is, once you have identified that there is little to no substantial reason to feel frustrated (or whatever the emotion), you can then begin to replace that thought process with something more empowering.

To achieve this you could simply think of something that is guaranteed to inspire gratitude, or just simply make you smile. You could use a number of the questions from the *Positive Morning Ritual* that we covered earlier within the chapter on *Self Worth* (see pages: 100 - 102), or you could simply just focus upon the laughter of your children or another loved one.

It could also be a certain place or memory that makes you smile or it could be anything else, even silly or "childish" in nature. Guess what? It really doesn't matter as long as it's not negative and it inspires some sense of joy and meaning.

When you have that picture in mind, focus on it as intensely as you can, and for as long as possible. Repeat this simple process as much as possible when first starting to break the old pattern of habitual frustration.

You can moderate it accordingly when you start to find it increasingly easier for the old negative programme to be replaced by the positive one. Will this totally eradicate these patterns overnight? No, probably not. But steadfast: *notable progress is born out of a process.* The new pattern will become natural and habitual through repetition, just as the old one did.

Of course, this is not only applicable for anger management but as mentioned; it can also be effective for a number of negative thought patterns including those of: type 2 fear, jealousy, envy, distrust, anxiety, depression, and so on.

Casual Question

Aside from this, there is yet another casual question that we can ask ourselves when having difficulty relaxing, or stilling the mind from endless thoughts.

That question is: "*I wonder what my next thought is going to be?*" And once you ask yourself this question, actually turn your attention inward and wait for the next thought; you will find that it takes a little longer than usual.

This can momentarily help to stop the incessant ramblings of the mind by stilling the thought process. In that moment one can experience pure self-awareness and *presence*. This is the awareness *behind* the awareness: void of thought and emotion.

Emotional Intelligence

Uncontrolled emotional states can be likened to hurricanes. They ravage through our cities of reason with no regard for our sense of logic.

Operating from this state our emotions can easily override our morals and values; as a result, caught in the moment we might say and do things that we later regret. By contrast, operating from a more positive and *emotionally intelligent* state, our morals and values can keep our emotions in check.

So, what is this attribute termed as *Emotional Intelligence*? In a nutshell; emotional intelligence is simply the awareness of, and ability to control, which emotions we experience in any given situation; along with which thought processes or situations may trigger them off.

We therefore develop a keen insight toward the array of thoughts and feelings (direct and indirect) associated with that emotion, and the type of actions that we take as a result.

Most professional sportspeople also realise the importance of this, as throughout their career many of them receive some level of emotional-management coaching.

This helps them to identify and conquer any negative emotions (mainly frustration and anger) which may arise during their game because it is essential that these negative emotions are minimized where possible, otherwise they may affect the sportsperson's performance.

A Physical Shift

As we briefly touched upon in the chapter of *Confidence,* another great technique which can be used to change a negative emotional state is simply to shift your physiology.

For instance, if you are feeling lowly or in a semi-depressed state it is likely that your physiology conveys this; your shoulders will be slightly hunched forward, your head held low and your breathing pattern shallow.

Change this physical state: start by sitting up straight and not slouching. Consciously change your depth and rhythm of breathing from chest (shallow) to abdominal (deep). When walking outside, force yourself to look the world in the eye as opposed to staring at the pavement. Do this even at the possible expense of tripping up or stepping in something undesirable.

If you are slouching around at home due to feeling negative, spontaneously get up and do some jumping jacks; shake off that negative energy and stand tall; then think of a time in your life that you were really empowered and hold that thought.

A shift in your *physiological* state can be an immensely powerful tool for changing an *emotional* state. This is simply because emotions and physiology are intrinsically linked together through our sympathetic nervous system.

Just as when you begin to physically slouch you may begin to feel tired and yawn, by contrast when you sit up straight (as when paying attention while learning something new for instance) you will naturally begin to feel more assertive because this alone will trigger your "energy-boosting hormones."

You will then begin to feel *even* more assertive, which will then stimulate the release of even more of these hormones and the cycle will naturally begin to build upon itself. Now when you are feeling lowly, you need not rely upon something external to elevate your mood; because with this simple technique *you have the power to do so.*

Initially it may feel slightly odd to force yourself into a different posture which counters the emotional state that you are experiencing; but if kept up on a regular basis its effectiveness to rapidly shift your emotional state is undeniable.

Researchers at Stanford University (17) also conducted a study on the effects that our physiology has on our mood, and the results were conclusive.

In one study, the researchers found that when people shifted their physiology from a withdrawn type of posture, and instead assumed a more expansive and assertive posture, their anxiety hormones decreased by 25 percent while their energy boosting hormones increased by 19 percent.

However, if you find yourself in a situation where you experience some kind of intense frustration and it is not appropriate for you to express it, along with consciously relaxing your posture to something less tense, you can always make use of the age old calming technique which still stands strong to this day: deep breathing and counting.

Ten Deep Breaths - Count to Ten

This is so simple yet so effective because by deep-breathing we are, obviously, increasing our intake of oxygen. And this oxygen goes straight to the brain and immediately helps to produce a calming effect. And by the time that we count to ten the initial wave of anger would most likely have passed.

The counting aspect itself is also a great diversion, because as we are focused on the counting of numbers we are diverting most of our immediate attention away from the situation at hand. Counting backwards from 100 can also help.

Our thoughts can direct our emotions because: energy flows where attention goes.

Through diligent self-awareness we learn a great deal about some of the underlying influences which determine our range of behaviour in certain circumstances. And with this knowledge we can then truly begin to consciously *redefine our limits and redesign our lives.*

But as important as *self-awareness* is upon our quest of *utilising more*, there is also another significant factor which ultimately determines much of our behaviour, and that is; *our beliefs.* Adopting a set of empowering beliefs is fundamentally essential for personal growth.

This is particularly true within the area of self development because, as earlier stated, many of us will seldom progress beyond our own opinions of ourselves; especially if those opinions are principally formed as the result of our own...

Chapter 10

LIMITING BELIEFS

"If you accept a limiting belief, then it will become a truth for you." – Louise L. Hay

One way to define the word "belief" is: *The blind acceptance of something that has not yet been proven as fact*. And this definition is commonly associated with an attitude of naivety.

However, on another level; a belief can also be defined as: *A feeling of certainty about what something means to us.* And it is this latter definition which provides the premise for this chapter.

When referring to beliefs, for the most part, I am not simply referring to the credulous blind acceptance associated with the first definition. But rather, I am referring to the deeper rooted core beliefs that we *all* have in varying degrees.

Whether these are cultural beliefs, religious beliefs, moral beliefs, societal beliefs, personal beliefs and so on; if they contribute, in some way, toward shaping our sense of identity as a person—which then determines how we see the world—then they are to be considered: c*ore beliefs.*

Over time; many of these beliefs are so repetitively and consistently reinforced and supported with countless biased

references, that they are now simply just accepted as fact; and
seldom questioned, if at all. Hence they subconsciously
influence how we make decisions on a daily basis.

Throughout this chapter, we will be shining the light on *limiting*
beliefs in particular; and why identifying and replacing them
with their empowering counterparts is so essential. Increasing
our awareness of even those subtle limiting beliefs, and thereby
exposing them for scrutiny, is an indispensable aspect of
personal growth and development.

> **"Increasing our awareness of even those subtle
> limiting beliefs and thereby exposing them for
> scrutiny is an essential part of personal growth."**
>
> #TOOSYY

The Role Our Beliefs Play

Beliefs gain power with references! Just what does this mean
exactly? It means that; the more things which we find to support
an idea, is the more likely that idea is to become an actual belief.
Every single belief that you have is only such because at some
point, knowingly or unknowingly, you have internalised a
number of references that support it.

A reference that supports a belief can be anything that you rely
upon to validate it. Put simply, the reference is usually the
"because" element. For instance, "I know (believe) that XYZ is
true *because…*"

Beliefs can, of course, be empowering *or* disempowering. Along
with shaping our identity; our beliefs about who we are, where

we fit in, and the meaning of life itself, are what give us our own sense of purpose and direction.

Playing a central role in our ability to evaluate the world around us; our beliefs shape the fabric of our values (our moral beliefs) and principles, along with what decisions we make and, therefore, what kind of actions we take.

They are the reason why some of us take massive action toward our goals and others take very limited, to no action at all. Being intimately connected to our level of optimism or pessimism, our beliefs are what determine what we think we can or can't achieve.

For this reason the core beliefs that we hold can be very important factors upon which we base any subsequent evaluations. They can influence our perception on a profound level, and carry with them the seed of tremendous power.

I remember once listening to an audio programme entitled: *Awaken the Giant Within,* by, Anthony Robbins (18). In this audio programme, Robbins tells the story of when he once interviewed the Yale professor and bestselling author, Bernie Siegel. According to Robbins, Bernie Siegel shared with him some of the work that he'd been doing with people that had multiple personality disorders.

Robbins, paraphrasing Siegel, said; "The beliefs that some of these individuals had—that they had become a different person—incredibly resulted in unquestioned commands to their nervous systems and this caused measurable changes in their biochemistry. Once the person with the 'multiple personality disorder' had changed personality; their body literally begun to change before the researchers eyes within a moment's notice."

Robbins goes on to say, "The person's eye colour would actually change—as their personalities changed, literally from brown into blue. Physical markings on their body would disappear or reappear; even diseases like high blood pressure or diabetes would come and go depending on that person's *belief,* as to which personality they were truly manifesting."

At first glance, although this may be a seemingly extreme example denoting the power of belief; it is also illustrative of its influence. However, on a simpler level, there are also many background beliefs that we unconsciously rely upon to make quick decisions every day; a type of which I like to refer to as: *The shortcut belief.*

Shortcut Beliefs

We often use shortcut beliefs in order to skip the protraction of considering the smaller details when making a decision. For instance, one of these shortcut beliefs could be: *expensive equals good quality,* which in many cases could be true; but is it always? In his book *"Influence! The Psychology of Persuasion"* (19), Dr. Robert Cialdini precisely illustrates this point.

He tells the story of a young shopkeeper who had been trying to sell some turquoise jewellery, in the peak of the tourist season, to fairly affluent tourists. These particular pieces of jewellery were of a decent quality for the price that she was asking, yet still she was having very little success with selling them.

The shopkeeper had already tried everything that she could think of, whether it was moving their location in the shop to a more central spot, telling her sales staff to promote the items as hard as possible, or authorising small discounts; still the outcome was poor.

In one last desperate attempt to sell the turquoise jewellery before she went on holiday, the owner scribbled a note instructing her head saleswomen to re-price all the items in the turquoise jewellery cabinet down to ½ price. She was hoping to shift this turquoise jewellery once and for all, even if this meant that it was at a loss.

A couple of weeks later, upon her return from holiday, the shopkeeper noticed that every bit of the turquoise jewellery had been sold: not surprisingly, as she thought that the prices had been reduced. She was then informed, much to her amazement, that not only had all the items of turquoise jewellery been sold, but they had actually been sold at *double* the price.

The reason was due to the head saleswomen misreading the owners scribbled "½" as a "2" and therefore everything in the cabinet had been sold for twice as much, and went twice as fast, than when listed for the original cheaper price.

Although, at first glance, this would seem relatively baffling; the reason for this was fairly simple. When the price was low the tourists saw the turquoise jewellery as poor to average quality, and therefore their interest in the merchandise was also fairly low.

On the other hand, once the prices were raised to double the amount the tourists relied upon a common societal belief to make their decision, and that belief was, "you get what you pay for." Put simply, *"expensive equals good quality,* and by contrast, *cheap equals poor quality."* Therefore they automatically believed that if the jewellery was expensive then it was of much better quality and something worth having.

Rather than undergoing the laborious task of extensive research into just how valuable turquoise jewellery was, on that occasion the tourists had simply used this shortcut belief to quickly evaluate its worth. After all; other than looking good, it must have been expensive for a reason right?

Many of us rely upon similar types of shortcut beliefs to evaluate things every day, as this way it's easier for us to make prompt decisions in a fast-increasing technologically advanced modern world. Some of these beliefs may be empowering and progressive; and others, disempowering and limiting.

In either case, becoming self-aware of those beliefs (whether shortcut, or other) that unnecessarily limit our potential can remove the associated blockages and open up new pathways. These new pathways are paramount toward us mentally, spiritually and physically *utilising more*.

Limiting Beliefs:

As limiting beliefs play such an essential role in what we believe to be possible and vice versa, throughout this section we will explore various forms. But first off: what exactly is a limiting belief?

A limiting belief is any type of belief that causes us to limit our self expression and potential. These beliefs can often confine us to "mental prisons of mediocrity" by fostering self doubts; and thus they greatly limit our ability to achieve notable success.

Success—by the way—does not have to be money-related, it could be in relation to health, personality, purpose, love, experience, adventure, marriage, contribution, family life, internal happiness or it can be your progressive realisation toward any of these things and much more.

The very belief that *"Success equals money"* is within itself a limiting one, because it keeps us looking at success as something which can only be bought; when in reality "success" can be found in many areas of one's life, some financially related and others not.

It is typically thought that many of our fundamental limiting beliefs were adopted before the age of ten. And since then they have provided the basis—that is to say, the point of reference— for a number of subsequent beliefs that have been "stacked" upon them, so to speak.

When these beliefs are foundational as such, as we established earlier, they are commonly referred to as *core beliefs.*

Core Beliefs

So what makes our core beliefs so important? Our core beliefs can play an essential role towards our mental, emotional and spiritual growth. Sometimes when these shift; we experience what we refer to as *an epiphany.*

Identifying those core beliefs which unnecessarily limit our potential in some way can be crucial for long-lasting results within the corresponding area.

This is because there may be times when we want to change something within our lives, but we are doing so by attempting to replace the *surface belief* concerning that thing. Therefore the results, if any, are often short lived. So what exactly do I mean here? Let's take a look at a short example to further illustrate this point.

Imagine a fictional character by the name of Harry. Harry is overweight simply due to overeating, and his reason (excuse) is: *he overeats whenever he feels bored.* Now although this may be perfectly valid for Harry, in actuality this may only be his belief on the surface. The *core belief* that is *really* causing him to overeat might be something totally different.

If Harry addresses the surface belief, and begins to occupy himself in order to alleviate his boredom, he may well experience some temporary results, but at some point he may still find himself overeating because the *core* belief (reason) has not yet been addressed.

Take a look at the following example, imagine the surface belief as number one (on top), and the core belief as number five (the foundation beneath it).

1. Harry says that he overeats because he is bored: The belief here; overeating is caused by boredom. (surface level)

2. By asking the right questions, we dig a little deeper and Harry admits that he is bored because he's lonely: The belief here; his overeating is a result of loneliness. (surface level)

3. We continue to dig deeper still, and Harry admits that he is lonely because he is a little shy and fears rejection: The belief here; his overeating, indirectly, is a result of his shyness and fear of rejection. (mid level)

4. Deeper still, and Harry confides that he is shy and fear's rejection because he doesn't feel accepted. The belief here: his overeating is really the result of him feeling as though he is not accepted somehow. (deeper level)

5. Again we dig deeper; and it turns out that Harry doesn't feel accepted because he doesn't feel as though he's "good enough." Ahh, *now this is the core belief.* (core level)

Harry is really overeating, not simply because he's bored (on the surface), but because he doesn't feel as though he's "good enough" as a person. He has therefore neglected his (health) discipline by giving up hope and adopting a type of "I don't care anymore" attitude. And this "I'm not good enough" belief is the *core* belief upon which the rest are stacked.

But when Harry identifies and replaces this core belief, by default, he undoubtedly and automatically changes the whole pattern. Sometimes what we think is the "problem," in actuality is only the surface behaviour or belief; the *real* issue at the core of that "problem" could actually be something else.

This is why it can be essential for us to identify and address some of these core beliefs in order for us to bring about some real and lasting results, otherwise it's likely that we keep going around in circles: not unlike the dog chasing his tail.

This "tail chasing effect" is also evident within Harry's situation, because the very act of him overeating (because he doesn't feel good enough), only makes him gain more weight, become even more unhappy with his appearance, and *still* continue to feel, "not good enough."

However, now that we have distinguished Harry's core limiting belief, he is now able to effectively address it. Harry is now beginning to realise that overeating—as a means of escapism from not feeling good enough—is actually what is reinforcing the same feeling (unworthiness) that he is trying to escape, by overeating in the first place.

When Harry truly realises this, the distinction alone causes the whole belief system to implode upon itself. And this naturally empowers him, on a profound level, to transform his eating habits; providing that he wishes to do so.

To add to this, by identifying the limiting belief at the core (instead of addressing boredom which was on the surface), Harry can now focus on some empowering ways to elevate his overall sense of *self-worth.* And this will have a positive knock-on-effect within many other areas of his life.

If we want those weeds to stop growing within our garden, pruning the tops alone obviously won't make a lasting difference; but *pulling them out from the root will.* The same goes for the "weeds" (limiting beliefs) which grow within the fertile garden of the mind. Sometimes, even just identifying what the limiting belief is at the core; is enough for it to begin to dissipate.

> "Sometimes, even just identifying what the limiting belief is at the core; is enough for it to begin to dissipate."
>
> #TOOSYY

Core Beliefs Further Explained

Although, in the example of Harry we discovered a *limiting* core belief, this of course does not make all core beliefs negative or disempowering; they are entirely neutral and many of us may have some empowering and positive core beliefs also.

However, it's fairly obvious that we usually never have a quandary with the positive type, as they are not those which typically prevent us from achieving our goals.

Whether empowering or disempowering, our core beliefs are simply those which shape our perception on a more intricate and deep-seated level.

They are like the sieves that we use to filter new information that we are exposed to. And this then determines what that new information will *mean* to us. Put simply, we see things through the lenses of our core beliefs.

This is why—contrary to popular "belief," a considerable amount of our beliefs are not always formed by *absolute* reality; but instead, they are formed because we persistently collect, and are more prone to notice, bias information which supports our already existing core beliefs.

Many of these beliefs were first introduced to us through the opinions, teachings and advice of our parents, relatives, school teachers or other authority figures throughout childhood.

But regardless, all beliefs including those at the core, first started out as seedlings, and if accepted, we then water those seeds by gathering supporting references. Farouk Radwan explained "the seed" best in his article: *How Beliefs are Formed* (20), when he wrote:

"The belief formation process starts when a seed is implemented in the person's mind. This seed could be a small remark made by an authoritative person, some advice given by a close friend, or even a phrase you heard from a complete stranger."

"Sam is really arrogant"
"You don't know how hard it was to pass that exam"
"The economy is getting tougher"

"These are perfect examples of seeds," continues Radwan, "At this point the belief is not yet formed, but as you experience different situations (references) that water the seed, it will grow and become a solid belief."

Farouk Radwan's examples are as true of core beliefs as they are general beliefs. The only difference being that a core belief is one that has been accepted as truth, which has then laid the foundation for many subsequent beliefs (references) which have been "stacked upon it".

Running Counter

Contrary to the common consensus, with a little persistence, earnestness and willpower, any limiting belief concerning one's ability can be uprooted and replaced fairly easily. And one of the most effective ways to achieve this is simply to get up and do the very things that prove those beliefs wrong.

Once we are actively aware of a limiting belief, the more experiences that we have which run counter to it, the easier it can be uprooted and replaced by an empowering alternative. However, sometimes, we will not have those experiences if we do not gather the requisite courage to push through the first veneer of the belief that is limiting us.

For instance, you may have the limiting belief, "I'm too shy to give a speech in public." And even though a part of you has always wanted to stand up and give that speech at a special occasion; you have continuously prevented yourself from doing so by accepting this belief.

An associate of mine who is normally quite reserved in character, borderline "shy," believed that he would be completely hopeless at public speaking. One day with a bit of encouragement he decided to confront this limiting belief, head on, by attending a toastmasters meeting as a guest of mine.

When he was called upon to speak, for the first time in his life he stood at the head of an audience; admittedly his nerves was evident for the first few seconds but then as he spoke, his words and delivery started flowing, more and more confidently.

In fact he discovered that he had a real flair and passion for it, which was evident for all to see. He had reversed his belief of being "shy and completely hopeless at public speaking," just by actively pursuing and experiencing a situation that ran counter to it. And as his confidence grew in that area, there was no space left for that old limiting belief.

Undoubtedly, not all of us may have such a seamless experience; but I am sure that you get the point here: *Take action!* Many of us have some extraordinary talents, yet we continue to shy away from the experiences that will develop and nurture them. And typically at the root of us doing so will be some sort of limiting belief concerning our ability.

If we truly wish to unlock our potential and begin *utilising more* of our capabilities, these limiting beliefs must first be identified and then duly replaced with their empowering counterparts. It serves no productive purpose for us to continue imposing them upon ourselves, or allowing others to impose theirs upon us.

Common types

So, what are some of the most common limiting beliefs? They are typically the justifications for many of the self imposed boundaries that we place upon ourselves, which prevent us from excelling. And the more that we verbally repeat them to ourselves and others, the more solidified they become. These are limiting beliefs (excuses) like:

"I'm not good enough," "I'm too old," "I'm too young," "I'm not good-looking enough," "I'm not smart enough," "I come from a dysfunctional family," "My past is holding me back,"

"Money is evil," "I can either be rich or spiritual, but not both," "The world is a bad place," "I can't make it without him or her," "I have bad luck," "It takes too long to change," "There's not enough good opportunities to go around," "You only get one lucky break in life," "If I do 'XYZ' then people will think I'm crazy," "Rejection means that I am not good enough as a person," "Failure is bad," and the list goes on.

This last limiting belief on the list, "Failure is bad," is one of the most limiting of all, as it prevents us from attempting new things. Many of the others on the foregoing list are actually by-products of this belief, and are therefore merely used as excuses to inadvertently justify it.

The belief that "failure is bad" is almost inseparable from the belief that "rejection is bad," the only difference being one of context. But if we constantly shy from new endeavours due to imaginary fear that we will fail, then we are also sacrificing many key opportunities to learn and grow.

Innumerable opportunities to learn and grow arise, *disguised* as failure. Because when we "fail" at something; that is often where we learn the most, as we naturally want to prevent it from happening again. Thus we become more diligent, taking nothing for granted, and in this regard a certain degree of "failure" keeps us on our toes.

The more times we get something "wrong" the closer we become to getting it "right." As per the common saying: *"fail your way to the top."* In addition to this, if all of the heart's desires were to be attained too easily, it's likely that over a period of time many of us would become complacent and lazy.

It has been documented that Thomas A. Edison made over one thousand attempts, and failed, before successfully finding the correct filament for his version of the electric light bulb. Allegedly, when questioned on this amidst his "failures," his reply was; "I am not discouraged because every wrong attempt discarded, is another step forward."

Edison understood that *failure is nothing but a stepping stone to success.* And this, needless to say, is a much more empowering perspective to adopt towards it.

Failure is not bad. It is an essential part of growth and learning. Great success is very often preceded by great failure, and in this regard failure is an inescapable prelude to noteworthy achievement.

The greater the failure the greater the coming success, you will experience one in direct proportion to the other. Remember the pendulum swing effect? Think about it, how would you truly appreciate success without first experiencing its opposite? Such is the law of contrast. One day you will say: *"I have mastered failure, but look at me now.*

Zig Ziglar once said that you can always tell how *high* a building is going to go by looking at how *deep* the builders set the foundation. And similarly, the height to which you will rise in life will nearly always be determined by the depth of your own personal foundation. You *are* that builder. And you are digging deep into the soil of your character by overcoming failure and adversity. And it is the person that you become by doing so, which determines the height to which your "building" will rise.

One of my favourite quotes is from the great motivational speaker and trainer, Les Brown: "*If you've never failed at anything, then you've never reached for a big enough goal, most people fail in life not because they aim too high and miss, but because they aim too low and hit.*"

The limiting belief that failure is bad along with its sibling, rejection is bad, also causes us to avoid situations of approaching and meeting new people; consequently we forfeit many networking opportunities.

As these types of beliefs can be the very foundations that we base our capabilities and confidence upon; we would be doing ourselves a great favour by identifying and replacing them with some empowering alternatives. Doing so is not as hard as you might think; in fact it's relatively easy once we have the correct strategy in place, as we will soon see.

Some other common beliefs that can block our progress are: "I am not worthy of success," "I can't become successful because I didn't finish school," "I am unlucky," or, "I have never done that before so it's not for me and I would be no good at it."

As with those earlier, all of these are limiting beliefs because they restrict us from taking action toward a certain goal: a goal that we could have easily achieved had we just got up and went for it.

Some people may feel that they have no such beliefs, and of course it may be possible that they don't. But still, on the other hand, this could be worth further scrutiny. Perhaps the very belief itself "*I don't have any limiting beliefs*" could, paradoxically, be exactly that: *a limiting belief.*

And the reason for this is that, dependent on the mentality of the individual, this could potentially lead to a glorified form of self denial, causing them to overlook other areas that may need development within their character.

References

Anytime that we experience something our brains are automatically hardwired to search for any supporting thoughts or beliefs. Of course, this is an entirely neutral process and how we make sense of the world around us by scanning, labelling and categorising new experiences through our mental database of supporting references. And this is why it's essential that we notice when this process is being fuelled by disempowering thoughts and beliefs that hold us back from excelling.

Once we find ourselves doubting our abilities in some way then—as we saw in the last chapter—we can counteract the process by thinking of an empowering thought. This will, at least, neutralise the doubt. For instance, if our thoughts are those of scarcity, we could replace them with thoughts of abundance.

When necessary, we must consciously interrupt the pattern of these disempowering thought networks. This *principle of association*, being how our brains are wired, is the exact reason why limiting beliefs can be so disempowering; as one limiting belief can spawn a whole host of others.

For example: an obstacle arises that blocks your path amidst some sort of venture; and for a split second you begin to doubt, by thinking something like "Maybe this won't work." The chances are that your mind will then automatically search for similar thoughts or beliefs to act as references.

One limiting belief then leads to the next, and before you know it, "Maybe this won't work" has become "It's not the right time anyway;" so on and so forth.

In the final part of this chapter we'll look at some simple and effective techniques to eliminate these limiting beliefs one by one. As a result we will also wave goodbye to procrastination.

Procrastination

When we procrastinate on taking action toward something, in order to make ourselves feel better we will usually create some sort of excuse to justify our reasons for "putting it off." But every time that we put something off, the tendency strengthens until it becomes almost customary to keep doing so. As a result we are likely to continue using the *same old excuses* to validate further procrastination.

However, the more that we use these *excuses* to defend our procrastination, the more that we will begin to find "references" that support them and voilà: the excuse of "I'm not quite ready yet," has congealed into an *actual limiting belief,* supported by a number of bias justifications.

Many of our limiting beliefs can actually be formed without too much effort on our part. However, what's ironic is; the lengths that we'll go to in order to defend these beliefs, when challenged, can far outweigh the time it took for us to form them in the first place.

The reason for this is because sometimes when we identify with these beliefs, they become linked to our very own sense of identity. Thus when they are challenged, on a subconscious level, a part of our identity is being challenged, and therefore the ego will step in to defend the assailment of its own conceptual construct. The late Algerian psychiatrist and philosopher, *Frantz Fanon*, put it best when he said:

"Sometimes People hold a core belief that is very strong. When they are presented with evidence that works against that belief, the new evidence cannot be accepted. It would create a feeling that is extremely uncomfortable called cognitive dissonance. And because it is so important to protect the core belief, they will rationalize, ignore and even deny anything that doesn't fit in with that core belief." And this is particularly true of those beliefs that contribute in some way to our sense of identity.

Now that we have explored limiting beliefs in considerable depth, they can be identified and exposed from every angle. And by this stage, presumably, we are well aware of what they are, the most common types, how they arise, when they arise, why they arise, the effects they have, and the mindsets which they produce. Now, let's turn our attention to...

Empowering Beliefs:

In this section we need not explore any exhaustive list of empowering beliefs, because empowering beliefs and productive perspectives are the basis of this entire book; as to provide some empowering alternatives that we can use to dispel many of the most common limitations that prevent us from progressing was the key intent behind its writing.

Problem vs. Challenge

On any journey, it's possible that we encounter various types of obstacles. However, these obstacles only really become "problems" if we *label* them as such. As a substitute for labelling something as a "problem," if we instead label it as a "challenge," we immediately gain a more empowered approach toward it.

From this viewpoint, any "challenge" simply becomes an opportunity for you to develop yourself into somebody even stronger and wiser than before, and you do so by overcoming it.

Just as *pushing weights* in the gym can help to increase our physical muscles: overcoming the challenge of *pushing through adversity* can also help to increase our "emotional muscles." This also promotes strong self-belief and self-confidence in the face of, seemingly, overwhelming odds.

In reality, all events that happen in life are completely neutral. The universe is indifferent to *moral* distinctions. It is us, as the observers, who label and interpret events as "good" or "bad." And these two concepts are solely based on our perceptions; which consequently frame our beliefs.

Nonetheless, every "negative" situation contains the possibility of something positive: an opportunity of some sort. Whether we notice this is merely dependent upon our perception toward it.

As a basic example: imagine you're in a situation where you have a lack of resources to handle it efficiently; although at first glance this could be seen as a "problem," your lack of resources could actually be *reframed* into an opportunity to *utilise more* of your potential. This is because the situation now forces you to become *even more* creative and resourceful with the little that you have. In this state of mind you will be more likely to spot a number of opportunities for expansion that others would overlook or disregard, due to their complacency.

When things are going well, it's all too easy to become lost in complacency—lazily content with our position and surroundings. On the contrary, if we are faced with a situation where "our back is against the wall" and we have insufficient resources; oftentimes, we will more readily hunt down the opportunities for expansion in the most prosaic of circumstances.

Put simply, we become more diligent, more creative and more aware. We begin *utilising more*. And as a result we are then able to make the most of near enough anything as a means to succeed. Any self made millionaire that started out void of financial backing would also testify to this fact.

Does this mean that we should enjoy having limited resources? No, not necessarily. But it's just a more empowering way to look at the same situation; as opposed to adopting the defeatist attitude.

Fuller Expression

As previously mentioned, within the chapter on *Balance;* "*Nature is always seeking fuller expression of itself.*" And as one with nature, so is *the mind.* In this regard, a great number of the predicaments that we experience are those which have been consciously, or unconsciously, created by ourselves. This is one of the many ways that the mind is seeking "fuller expression" because it then has a challenge to overcome.

We typically then become more experienced, capable, stronger, wiser, and in short we become more "in-tune" with our *inner resources* of power. Furthermore, when faced with a challenge of some sort we then have an opportunity for a powerful reversal. We have a chance to exercise and demonstrate our ability to handle whatever arises.

Overcoming a challenge—and gaining wisdom and strength throughout the process—automatically increases our self-esteem and confidence. It is then likely that we knowingly or unknowingly express this heightened level of self-belief within other areas of our lives: seeking fuller expression.

The naked truth is that: for the human mind, *any obstacle can be utilised as an opportunity for expansion.* And that, in itself, is one of the ultimate empowering beliefs.

Doubt your Doubts

Now, let's get into some simple exercises that we can use to identify and replace a number of those limiting beliefs with their empowering counterparts.

But before we begin, you may remember the forthcoming point from earlier within this book; nonetheless, I would like to reiterate it again here: *If you question anything enough, eventually you will begin to doubt it.*

And this can be applied just as well to your doubts as it can with anything else; question them enough and you will begin to, *doubt your doubts.* These doubts are, of course, nothing other than limiting beliefs. Please also bear this in mind that other than having an objective approach, there are two additional qualities which are necessary for you to adopt toward these simple exercises, and they are: *absolute honesty,* and *earnest willingness* to make progress.

If you approach these exercises with anything short of these two qualities within mind and heart, then the results that you attain will reflect that. With that said, let's now identify and replace some of these limiting beliefs:

1. Firstly, turn off the television, along with any other distractions; this exercise will take only 10-to-15 minutes.

2. Think of a goal that you want to achieve and then write it down for more clarity, be vivid and specific.

3. Now write down the top three limiting beliefs that you feel are preventing you from achieving this. These can be from the list earlier (see pages 222 - 223), or they can be any others that come to mind. (Again, be as objective and honest with yourself here as possible).

(Tip: if you cannot think of your top three limiting beliefs then ask yourself; what are the *top three* excuses that I use when I don't take action toward something? These three excuses will usually be directly in line with the three limiting beliefs. In fact, as we saw earlier, those excuses could be how those beliefs got there in the first place.)

Now, for each of these three beliefs, write down the answers for the following two questions:

1) What has this belief cost me so far?

2) What will this belief cost me in 5 years time?

The aim here is to see exactly what these limiting beliefs are denying you, along with all the opportunities that you may have turned down because of them. Imagine ... no, I mean *really* imagine ... where you would be; and all you would have achieved by now, if not for these beliefs.

However, now that you have honestly identified them, it's time to begin the process of questioning. You can use those below or think of some of your own:

1) How is this belief true?

2) Where and when did I even get this belief?

3) Was the person I learned this belief from worth modelling in this area, were they producing results?

4) Why isn't this belief a ridiculous one?

5) Do I really want to keep limiting my potential with this belief?

6) What will it cost me if I don't change this belief?

7) What will it cost my family if I don't change this belief?

Once you have taken some time to seriously question these beliefs, you will notice that you are beginning to doubt them and they will begin to loosen their "grip" on you.

The next step is to write down your top five empowering beliefs. For instance, "I am here on earth for a greater purpose," or "I can achieve anything that I put my mind to," or "My mind is infinite, and one with the creative source of the universe," or "I would not be faced with a situation if I couldn't handle it," so on and so forth.

Of course, you do not have to use any of these; you can just as easily create a list of your own that works for you.

Feel the certainty and positivity associated with these empowering beliefs as you *write them down*. The purpose here is to increase your *awareness* of these empowering beliefs so you naturally begin to use them more often. You cannot make good use of something that you are not aware of.

As simple as this exercise is; do not fall into the trap of equating simple with ineffective, as that is also a limiting belief. Oftentimes we may tend to overlook the simple things in pursuit of complexities so that we may feel more intelligent, and in doing so we unnecessarily complicate things.

Once you have discovered some of your most empowering beliefs, the final phase of this exercise is to:

1) Take a few minutes to write down *three* ways that you could strengthen them. Whether it's writing them down and looking at them regularly throughout the day; using them as affirmations each morning and night; frequently visualising yourself succeeding as a result of them; reading, watching or listening to more empowering books, DVDs, CDs, et cetera.

2) Think of other areas in your life where you may have demonstrated these beliefs. If you have these empowering beliefs in those areas, then can you transfer them to another? Yes. Absolutely! You can do anything that you put your mind to! Let nobody convince you otherwise: *EVER!*

So, throughout the *Third Cornerstone of Potential* we have increased our level of *self-awareness*; and are now better-equipped to identify and replace our *limiting beliefs*. We are thus no doubt *utilising more* of our true greatness.

We all have approximately 1440 minutes every day, and on average most of us are awake for roughly 960 of them; surely we can dedicate even 20 of those minutes to these types of exercises which will greatly enhance our lives in every area.

After all, our lives will not change significantly by *passively* reading. Our lives will change by *actively* reading, and this means *following through* on that which is read.

With that said, we now know that our beliefs can greatly influence the perceptions we hold toward things, and how we perceive reality can either propel us toward, or away from, identifying our true purpose and utilising our abundance of latent potential.

Therefore, it is now imperative that we enter into the final section of this book. All paths thus far, have led us to this point. We will now crossover into the *Fourth Cornerstone of Potential*; wherein, we will reach what is considered to be the apex of the information within this publication. See you on the other side.

The End of Part Three

THE FOURTH CORNERSTONE OF POTENTIAL

Perceiving More

Chapter 11

THE MAP

"It is one of the commonest of mistakes to consider that the limit of our perception is also the limit of all there is to perceive." – C.W. Leadbeater

Within this fourth and final cornerstone we will explore some of the fundamental aspects which contribute toward human perception, along with how we tend to filter information and how this affects our view of, what we call, reality. This is of stupendous importance because in essence: *perception is the key to a heightened state of consciousness!*

Having a better understanding of this not only enables us to begin *perceiving more*, but it also helps with safeguarding us from any untoward manipulation; particularly from those who do have an understanding of these workings, but use them selfishly.

We have now entered into the only section of this book which is not exclusively related to how we view ourselves, as it focuses more on the broader scope of how we view *reality* on the whole.

If this type of information is new to you, it's likely that it may result in a paradigm shift toward your advancement. This fundamental shift in perception may then awaken you to a level of acuity not yet experienced, and thus, once keenly entertained, a new way of being emerges.

Reality

Typically, that which we refer to as reality is based upon how we perceive the world. But our perception is influenced by the *meanings* that we attribute to our experiences, that is to say, what we make things *mean* to us. We all know that a single experience can *mean* different things to different people. But nonetheless, these meanings are principally coloured by our individual (or joint) beliefs, values, morals, memories, environments, upbringings, our cultures and so forth. As a consequence, our views are naturally *biased* by these factors.

How we see the world in our mind's eye is similar to a type of "mental map" of reality. It is *not* reality itself, but our *interpretation* of it. However, many of us are relying upon a fairly limited version of this "mental map" to make sense of the world. And this is because we rely upon the equally limited aspects of our perception (the five senses) to create and support it.

Now of course, there are a growing number of people that are keenly aware of what some call *the sixth sense* (which is typically responsible for things that cannot be solely attributed to the five senses such as: hunches, premonitions, intuition, gut feelings, telepathy, telekinesis and so on), but for the most part what many of us term as "reality," is based upon the— fundamentally essential, but still—fairly limited information that is perceived through the five senses: taste, touch, smell, sight and audio.

As we'll see in the next chapter, the rationale for this is that many of us have never *really* been taught about what is now known as extrasensory perception (ESP), let alone how to utilise it.

As a result; many people negate its importance, and sometimes even its existence. They refuse to acknowledge anything outside of the physicality's that are commonly perceived through the five senses, and this restricts their awareness from perceiving that which is beyond the tangible forms of reality.

This then begs the question; is there a difference between absolute reality, and our general perception of it? The logical answer here would have to be; *yes there is.* And although there are numerable reasons behind this logic, at this stage we'll touch upon just two of them.

1) The first reason is that; as we know, the material world—which many of us believe to be fully tangible and solid (a brick wall for instance)—is merely made up of atoms.

But an atom is far from solid. It has been common knowledge among scientists and quantum physicists for some time that atoms predominantly consist of "empty" space: *99.9999999999999 percent empty space.*

In layman's terms, as a mild illustration; imagine that the nucleus (at the centre) of an atom was our sun: the electron could then be likened to the planet earth revolving around it, but at a much faster speed; with all that "space" in between. It's essentially a similar principle on both the macro and micro level.

In fact; if the nucleus of the simplest atom (being hydrogen) were *really* the size of the sun; then the distance between the electron and the nucleus would be around 1300 times larger than the distance between the earth and the sun now, which is approximately 93 million miles (if we multiply 93 million by 1300 we get a total of: 120900000000 miles of empty space).

This gives you a macrocosmic idea of how much "empty" space (which is really filled with energy: just as the empty space in between you and this book) is within a single hydrogen atom.

Yet these atoms, which are mostly "empty" space, are responsible for what we *believe* to be a *solid* and dense physical reality. And of course, this "solid reality" is simply consequent to how we are *perceiving* reality to be.

2) The second reason that there is a difference between *absolute* reality and our general perception of it is because; when consciously experiencing something, we typically tend to filter that event through a type of "internal processing system." This means that we attribute a *meaning* to that experience based on the various factors earlier mentioned (our beliefs, values, memories, and so on).

This is at the basis of us *perceiving more* or indeed, perceiving less: either one is primarily the result of how we are *filtering* the information that we are exposed to.

Ultimately, the entire human experience is a subjective one. And this is because we tend to filter (and bias) what is really a neutral experience by *deleting, distorting* and *generalising* the information which is being received; so that it may coincide with our own perception, and *meaning*, of reality.

Let's take a moment to briefly explore the significance of these three major filters, and how they apply to human perception.

Deletion:

Deletion can also be seen as selective awareness. A type of deletion is even occurring for you right now: as you read this book; that is where you're attention is, selectively. Thus (unless you are utilising Hakalau, as we learnt of in *Balance*), you are less aware of the other factors present within your environment.

We can also further illustrate this concept of "deletion" by using another simple example. Imagine that I entered a room which was occupied with various things (objects, people, etc.); my attention would naturally fall upon whatever was most interesting or relevant to me. This could be anything from a bottle of water, if I were thirsty, to a familiar face. Or it could just simply be whatever caught my attention based on my mindset at the time.

If you were to follow me into that room, your attention would also naturally be drawn to that which interested you, at the time, which could be something entirely different. Now, although we both went into the same room and our senses were exposed to the same "raw data," logically our attention would be drawn to the factors most in line with our dominant interests; while the other aspects present would be ignored, at least momentarily. And this is a form of deletion (similar to Greg's situation that we read about earlier in: *Self Awareness*).

Infinite Possibilities

When we experience a situation, there are *infinite possibilities,* however, our attention naturally gravitates toward the factors which tally with our beliefs, morals, values, interests' etc., and we ignore and disregard (delete) the other factors present which do not.

The thing here is that, when we fail to recognise the *many possibilities* of any experience, we also overlook the opportunities for growth and expansion concealed within them.

If you remember back in the opening chapter we touched upon *"The Present of Presence,"* because many of us delete (block out) things from present awareness due to being disproportionately focused on past or future events; and thus we can tend to severely limit our perspective in the *"Now."* However, deletion can also occur when we are recalling a memory.

Deletion & Memory

Deletion is not only applicable to present tense; but it also contributes, on a very basic level, toward how we store and filter our memories. If I were to recall a memory of an event, at which we were both present, I would naturally recall to mind the most prominent features of the event according to *me*: automatically disregarding those not so prominent.

On the other hand, if *you* were to recall a memory of the same event, then there's a chance that your prominent features would be slightly different to mine, as you would also naturally filter the memory, from your point of view, deleting the aspects not so important to you.

Selective Awareness & the Conscious Mind

In essence, deletion is an essential attribute of the conscious mind. If we were unable to delete certain things from our awareness, we would not have the ability to focus on one thing at a time. Also, if too much information was constantly coming through the senses at any one time, this could cause an information overload and result in confusion.

From this viewpoint, deletion is not a negative trait but an entirely neutral and essential one. The key here is learning how to better utilise this selective awareness, in order that we may turn it on, or off, at will.

Of course, there are times when we may need to selectively focus on one thing only, but by contrast, *there are also times when it would be far more beneficial for us not to limit our perspective, thus staying open to all possibilities.*

Thus, instead of seeing things from the angle of just one spoke on the bicycle wheel, we see the whole wheel.

A Noteworthy Role

Since "Deletion" greatly determines what level of awareness we have at any one moment, this one of the *three major filters* plays a noteworthy role toward increasing our perception.

Our selective awareness is accountable for whether we "think outside the box" or remain within the confines of a set paradigm, consequently failing to utilise a great deal of potential opportunities.

Ultimately, the present moment has unlimited opportunities, but we limit those when we take on any one *set* view.

As we fall victim to needless rigidity we thus fail to acknowledge the many other perspectives and possibilities present. And this can be the bane, when it comes to us *perceiving more*. With that said; the second of the major filters is known as…

Distortion:

Distortion is how we attribute meaning to an experience via our *interpretation* of it. Have you ever witnessed a scenario where one picture can have five different meanings to five different people? Of course, this is because each person would have been interpreting the same information, differently.

In essence, our experiences are entirely neutral; it is our mental distortions of them that render them as good or bad, right or wrong, etc. William Shakespeare put this best when he said: *"Nothing is either good or bad, but only thinking makes it so."*

When we "distort" experiences, we are mentally tailoring those events to best suit our own perspective and, once again, we filter these in line with our beliefs, values, morals, memories, environments, upbringings, our cultures and so forth.

Put simply, what determines how we feel is never the experience itself, but rather the *meaning* that we attribute to it (how we are distorting it).

"What determines how we feel is never the experience itself; but rather, the meaning that we attribute to it."

#TOOSY

When we distort something, we are interpreting information differently to how others might view the same experience. Similar to deletion; distortion also plays a pivotal role in how we perceive things because it's how we give things meaning; thus determining the kind of relationship that we have with them.

However, as with any type of behaviour over which we are in control, our distortions of reality can contribute to our benefit or, by contrast, to our detriment.

Needless to say, there are countless examples of our distortions (as we give some sort of meaning to nearly everything based on our perception of it); but one such favourite of mine is "The Forer Effect," named after the psychologist Bertram R. Forer (21).

In one of his most well known experiments Forer selected a number of students; all of which came from *various backgrounds and belief systems.* Each student was then told that they would receive a detailed and individual assessment of their own personality.

Once they had received their "detailed personality assessments;" each student then went off to privately read, and score their assessment on its accuracy. Once they had all completed this and their papers had been handed in to Forer, the results revealed that the students had marked their assessments with an average score of 4.3 out of 5.

I'm sure that as you're reading this; you too would probably agree that 4.3 / 5 is a fairly high score? And to achieve this score, these detailed and *individual* personality assessments surely must have been fairly accurate right? Wrong! There was a slight catch; after all, this was an experiment.

So what was the catch? Well, it was rather simple; although each of the students thought they were getting *individualised* personality assessments, Forer had actually given them all *the exact same description*. And what's more; he had simply compiled this description from various horoscopes of the day and time.

Even though they all thought that their assessments had been personalised, at the end of the experiment it was revealed to the students that they had all been given the exact same description. And then it was revealed that despite this, they had all marked their assessments as nearly 90 percent accurate. Of course when this was exposed, the responses of the students were those of complete bewilderment.

This experiment, originally conducted by Forer in 1948, has been repeated hundreds of times since and has still maintained an average score of 4.3 / 5. One of the most recent times it has been conducted, on national television, was by the renowned hypnotist and showman, Derren Brown.

Nonetheless, the outcome is usually the same: people from various backgrounds, cultures, belief systems and even different countries are told that they will receive personalised assessments of their character, but then they are all given the exact same description. They go off to read it, and mark it, in private; and the majority of them rate it as a near enough accurate description of their personality.

"Why?" you might ask. And the reason for this is that; apart from the information within the assessment being *artfully vague*, those who took part had also, to some degree, *distorted* the information to best suit their view of themselves. Here is what the original Forer assessment said to those who took part:

"You have a great need for other people to like and admire you. You have a tendency to be critical of yourself. You have a great deal of unused capacity which you have not turned to your advantage. While you have some personality weaknesses, you are generally able to compensate for them. Your sexual adjustment has presented problems for you. Disciplined and self-controlled outside, you tend to be worrisome and insecure inside. At times you have serious doubts as to whether you have made the right decision or done the right thing. You prefer a certain amount of change and variety and become dissatisfied when hemmed in by restrictions and limitations. You pride yourself as an independent thinker and do not accept others' statements without satisfactory proof. You have found it unwise to be too frank in revealing yourself to others. At times you are extroverted, affable, and sociable, while at other times you are introverted, wary and reserved. Some of your aspirations tend to be pretty unrealistic. Security is one of your major goals in life."

At this point you might say, "Well, that assessment is fairly vague anyway," and you'd be absolutely right. However, that is only further proof of the distortion of the information, by those who took part in the experiment.

Had those individuals not been so preoccupied with distorting the information to fit in with their own perspectives of themselves (as most of us would have done in similar circumstance); they would have effortlessly noticed just how terribly vague the description was. Therefore, they wouldn't have been as surprised (as they were) to later find out that they had all been given the exact same information within the assessment.

As earlier mentioned; the assessments, that Forer provided those who took part in the experiment, had been comprised from the information within various horoscopes of that day and time. For this reason alone, it should come as no surprise to you that it's also the same type of *artfully vague language* which is used within many of the mainstream horoscopes of today.

However, many of us will typically *distort* the information within mainstream horoscopes in order for it to apply to whatever is happening within our lives at any given moment.

By stating this; am I then, indirectly, negating the link between the celestial bodies and human nature? No I am not! I am simply referring to the ambiguity of the cleverly indistinct language patterns; used within many current, commercialised, horoscopes.

At this time it should be clear to see how our mental *deletions* and *distortions* of an experience (based on our beliefs, values, morals, memories, etc), can indeed affect our perception. Now let's move on to the third of the major filters: *Generalisation.*

Generalisation:

Our generalisations account for our "All" or "Never," distinctions. This is where we make blanket generalisations, usually based on a few previous experiences. You may remember the example of the turquoise jewellery in the last chapter, where the tourists equated *expensive* with *good quality.*

Those tourists (as many of us do) were *generalising* that "expensive equals good quality." Many of us generalise things based on our memories of similar experiences in the past; "*This meant that then, so it means that now.*" Put simply; our generalisations are the basis for all archetypes, evolving into stereotypes.

Our Generalisations of events make it easier for us to mentally categorise those events without having to meticulously scan through all of the individual details. Although an entirely neutral process, our generalisations of events can also be one of the major reasons for our prejudices (pre-judgments) of certain person's, places or things.

There are cultural related generalisations i.e., the "Americans" are *generally* flamboyant and extraverted; or, the "English" are *generally* subdued and love to drink tea.

Then there are age related generalisations i.e., (*all*) young people like to party; money related generalisations i.e., money buys happiness; gender based generalisations i.e., all women are smarter than men; social-class generalisations i.e., wealthy people are pompous; aesthetic generalisations i.e., if it *looks* good for you then it *is* good for you, moral generalisations concerning what's good and what's bad; and the list goes on.

Furthermore, a generalisation is when we place someone or something into a box based on familiar, but limited, aspects of information. As a result we then tend to categorise things without much scrutiny and are therefore more likely to make snap-computes; often disregarding the minutiae, along with other people's points of view.

Needless to say, as already mentioned, although our generalisations can make it easier for us to rationalise new information, taken to the extreme they are the starting point of all stereotypes.

So why is any of this important? Once again; it's important because when we delete, distort and generalise information, this is how we filter and interpret a great deal of experiences. And as previously stated it's our perception of something which determines our behaviour toward it.

The forthcoming phrase is of stupendous magnitude and once it is truly understood a myriad of opportunities will present themselves and new doors will begin opening from every angle; moreover, you will begin noticing the doors that were already open, where you had not before:

Every experience has unlimited possibilities, but we limit those possibilities when we rigidly attach ourselves to any one set point of view.

Override the Process

The very act of us becoming more aware of when we are deleting, distorting or generalising information, can then enable us to consciously override the process.

When and where necessary, we can do this by forcing ourselves to look at the same situation from a widened perspective, acknowledging and appreciating the various elements that are present. This is undoubtedly where we make the most of any experience, and thus we begin *perceiving more*.

So just to recap; we do not experience reality directly, but merely our *perception* of it. And our perception of reality will always be fairly limited from the whole, because we filter (by way of deleting, distorting and generalising) information in accordance with our beliefs, values, morals, memories, environments, upbringings, our cultures and so forth. All of this then contributes to our mental "map" of reality.

Outdated Maps

The Map is our internal representation of reality, that is to say, how we compute information within our mind's eye. This does not make it *the* reality, but merely *our interpretation* of it.

For example; a road map is a powerful interpretation of the territory, but it is not the territory itself. A menu is a powerful interpretation of a meal, but it is not the meal itself. And likewise our *internal maps* are a (sometimes) powerful *interpretation* of reality, but not reality itself.

Remember; all human experience is subjective via perspective; and this is based on the one doing the perceiving.

If we are using "outdated maps" (interpretations) to make sense of new experiences, then it's no surprise that as a result, we may not make the best decisions when doing so.

The old methods, with which we approached situations in the past, are not necessarily the way we should approach them now. "Well that's fairly obvious," you might say; and you'd be right: in theory, it is quite obvious. But what's more obvious is how many of us (due to habit) *still* inflexibly stick to methods learnt long ago when faced with new challenges.

> "All human experience is subjective via perspective; and this is based on the one doing the perceiving."
>
> #TOOSYY

To metaphorise this; imagine if I were to drive a car that had an inbuilt satellite navigation system, "Sat Nav," from the year 1999, the chances are that the virtual map may be slightly outdated and not an entirely accurate reflection of how the city is today.

And obviously, this would be due to the fact that the city itself is constantly evolving with new monuments, roads, and routes, (etc.) being built, destroyed or remodelled. Therefore, directions which the Sat Nav would provide in order for me to get from point A to point B in 1999; would not necessarily be the most efficient route to get me to that location in 2013.

But never mind the map of a Sat Nav, many of us could also apply this point of view to our own "mental maps" of reality; that is to say, how we map things out within our minds.

This is particularly evident when we use *outdated approaches* toward new challenges, or rigid perspectives toward new insights.

Some of these approaches may even be considered traditional or conservative yet, in essence, they lack the flexibility required to solve certain issues in today's world.

Likewise, a number of these perspectives may have been fore-necessary and served us quite well a decade ago, *when we were that person*; but as we have evolved since then, many of the old methods-of-approach have become defunct, yet we cling to them in fear of change.

But in the ever-changing, fast moving, modernised world of today, which is constantly evolving, we must periodically reinvent ourselves through realistic inner-enquiry, diligent self-awareness, focused determination, and *bold new action*.

We must consider and utilise fresh perspectives—as you are doing right now by simply reading this book;—otherwise, consequently we may fail to move with the times and our methods of approach to new challenges carry the stale demeanour of times long past.

With these new insights, we can significantly increase the results that we manifest within all areas of our lives.

In the next chapter, we will explore the most profound and powerful resource available to human beings: a resource so powerful that its true magnitude is beyond logical comprehension.

But in order for *you* to begin utilising this *stupendous* resource to a fuller degree, it would first require that you have, at least, a basic understanding of its faculties. And for this reason it would be highly advisable that you...

Chapter 12

MIND YOUR MIND

"The greatest weapon in the hands of an oppressor is the mind of the oppressed." – African Proverb

B efore we get into the information within this chapter, I would like to first state that some of the concepts examined herein may challenge the "normal" preconceived ideas that some of us hold toward such subject matters.

The core intention here is not to impress the reader with breadth, nor depth, of knowledge; nor is it to come across as eloquently profound or technical.

But as this fourth cornerstone of potential is centred on heightening perception, the purpose of the information herein is to stretch the perspective of the reader beyond the confines of everyday thought patterns; particularly if you, as the reader, are coming across this information for the first time.

Imagine the information itself as a "signpost." It is not the post, per se, that is of utmost importance; but more so the direction to which it is pointing. And in this case, that signpost is pointing toward a shift in consciousness as we begin upon the path to *perceiving more*. With that said; if you are fairly new to these concepts, please read on with an open mind.

Source Energy

For many thousands of years, through deep inner inquiry, a great number of philosophers and sages have come to the realization that at the core of existence, there is one fundamental source of energy, which we are all intrinsically connected to.

Many of us may refer to this *source energy* by a number of different names, which are usually dependent upon our culture or belief system. For example; nowadays within the physics' community, and also within the scientific community, it's sometimes referred to as *The Unified Field.*

In Spiritual Philosophy it has been referred to as: The All, Universal Consciousness, God Consciousness, Spirit Force, Chi, or Divine Love. And in various religious teachings: Advaita, Brahman, Tao, Nirvana, Heaven, or even just simply; God.

Of course, there are many other names, titles and attributes that have been attached to this *source energy*; however, in reality the name is only relevant as far as it resonates with the individual.

Whatever name, or adjective, that we decide to attach to it; one thing is for sure: somewhere deep within our very being, unexplainably, we innately sense our connection with it. Our deep-rooted yearning to become more aware of—and more at one with—this infinite source of energy is the underlying basis for all forms of spirituality.

It is also now commonly accepted, by most conventional scientists, that all sense of being—and consciousness— subsequently arises from this *source energy*: thought, by them, to have been created during the Big Bang of 13.5 million years ago.

Albert Einstein—who coined the phrase "unified field"—also told us that "everything is energy", and that we are a part of *"the whole,"* nevertheless, this truth observed by Einstein merely echoed the most ancient of spiritual and philosophical teachings.

This source energy is like a great *Universal Mind,* in the sense of: *an Infinitely Vast Creative Intelligence,* of which we are an expression. Furthermore, it is the *whole* of which we are a part. And in accordance with the most basic laws of nature; a part must reflect that from which it came: with the only distinctions being those of degree.

This is the profound truth of the ancient teachings. We are all interconnected, not just as humans, but to all of Nature; ultimately everything in the Universe. And although the physical body creates the illusion that we are separate, beyond this illusion we are separate from nothing because at the source, *everything is energy.*

Therefore, all attributes are present within us at all times in their potential form: *energy.* However, to manifest these we must bring ourselves into vibrational harmony with the nature of them, and this can be achieved through the creative power of our thoughts and emotions.

As our thoughts are what determine our actions, a man or woman essentially becomes nothing other than that which is in alignment with their most dominant thought patterns. Hence the common biblical saying; "As a man thinketh in his heart, so is he." *Thoughts become things!* But this is to pose yet another question: If we are all so intrinsically connected to this infinite *Universal Mind*, then why is it that we only use such a small fraction of our mental potential?

The Ten Percent Theory

It has often been said that as human beings, we only use approximately 7-to-10 percent of the human brain. While there have been various arguments made for, and against, this; I would not disagree in the slightest that the brain has much more to offer.

The human brain is like the central computer which manages all of the bodily functions by way of the nervous system. It has been estimated to have anywhere between 80-to-120 billion (yes, billion) *neurons*. And these neurons have branches which are estimated to connect with each other, at up to 500 trillion points. These points where neurons connect to *one another* are called *synapses*.

Neurons (nerve cells) are typically responsible for transmitting vast amounts of information within the brain by chemical and electrical signalling. Certain signals, that form memories and thoughts, move through an individual neuron by way of an electrical charge.

When a charge reaches a synapse, it typically triggers a tiny burst of certain chemicals, and these chemicals are referred to as *neurotransmitters*. It is the neurotransmitters which then travel between synapses transmitting the relevant signals.

The material complexities of the brain are extremely profound and although a number of its material functions are generally understood by the Neuropsychologists and Cognitive Scientists of today, it would be fair to say that these properties were considerably less understood a century ago within the field of western based brain research.

The theoretical conclusion that we only use 10 percent of the brain's *mass* is one that was reached—in the west—within the late nineteenth to early twentieth century.

Although there were a few contributing factors (including the experiment of psychologist Karl Lashley which found that animals could re-establish functions that they had lost, after he removed substantial parts of their brains) that lead to this conclusion, one of which was that; some scientists thought that only 10 percent of the human brain had neurons, and that the remaining 90 percent consisted mostly of *Gilal Cells.*

At the time, it was believed that these Gilal Cells had no particular function, rendering them useless. So, as a consequence it was also believed that because these cells accounted for approximately 90 percent of the brain, and they had no (known) function, that we must only utilise the remaining 10 percent of the brain. And the 90 percent was, therefore, considered to be unutilised.

However, as neuroscience has evolved considerably since this hypothesis came about at the turn of the century, this idea has been largely discredited. Due to much updated technology and research, neuroscientists have now found that these Gilal Cells have at *least* four key functions within the brain, such as (1)

surrounding the neurons and holding them in place, (2)
supplying vital nutrients and oxygen to the neurons, (3)
insulating the neurons from one another and (4)
destroying harmful pathogens and removing dead neurons.

Needless to say, this alone challenges the theory that we only
use 10 percent of our brain, or at the least it proves that we use
more than 10 percent of our brain's *mass:* reason being; this
portion of the human brain once thought to be null and void, in
actuality, is incredibly far from it.

To add to this, in the book; *Mind Myths*: *Exploring Popular
Assumptions About the Mind and Brain* (22) *, "*
neuroscientist Barry Beyerstein sets out various points of
evidence refuting this 10 percent idea, some of which are as
follows:

   I.   "Studies of brain damage: If 90% of the brain is
normally unused, then damage to these areas should not
impair performance. Instead, there is almost no area of
the brain that can be damaged without loss of abilities.
Even slight damage to small areas of the brain can have
profound effects."

   II.   "Evolution: The brain is enormously costly to the rest of
the body, in terms of oxygen and nutrient consumption.
It can require up to twenty percent of the body's
energy—more than any other organ—despite making up
only 2% of the human body by weight. If 90% of it were
unnecessary, there would be a large survival advantage
to humans with smaller, more efficient brains. If this
were true, the process of natural selection would have

eliminated the inefficient brains. By the same token, it is also highly unlikely that a brain with so much redundant matter would have evolved in the first place."

III.   "Brain imaging: Technologies such as Positron Emission Tomography (PET) and functional magnetic resonance imaging (FMRI) allow the activity of the living brain to be monitored. They reveal that even during sleep, all parts of the brain show some level of activity. Only in the case of serious damage does a brain have "silent" areas."

IV.   "Localisation of function: Rather than acting as a single mass, the brain has distinct regions for different kinds of information processing. Decades of research have gone into mapping functions onto areas of the brain, and no functionless areas have been found."

V.   "Micro structural analysis: In the single-unit recording technique, researchers insert a tiny electrode into the brain to monitor the activity of a single cell. If 90% of cells were unused, then this technique would have revealed that."

VI.   "Neural disease: Brain cells that are not used have a tendency to degenerate. Hence if 90% of the brain were inactive, autopsy of adult brains would reveal large-scale degeneration."

In addition to these points from Beyerstein; a further source, on Wikipedia, wrote:

"In the October 27, 2010 episode of *MythBusters*, the hosts used magneto-encephalography and functional magnetic resonance imaging to scan the brain of someone completing a complicated mental task. Their findings showed that well over 10% of the participant's brain was active at once."

It is perceptible that many of these points offer reasonable evidence against the 10 percent claim. However; for the most part they seem to be referring strictly to the brain's *mass*; and not necessarily the *capability* of that mass. What does this mean? In short it means that while we may absolutely use more than 10 percent of the brain's *physical material*, this does not indubitably demonstrate that we use this "material" to its *fullest capability*.

"And, why do we not use the brain to its fullest capability?" Well, the answer here is rather simple; because, in most cases, we were never taught to. And resultantly—as we covered within the last chapter—many of us accept only what can be perceived through the five senses, as *absolute* reality.

This means that the brain only has to utilise as much power as necessary in order to maintain this (comparatively) basic level of perception. For instance; even though many of us, at some point, have experienced a spontaneous "hunch" or mild premonition (i.e. you think of someone, and then suddenly the phone rings and it's them), typically, we'll attribute many of these occurrences to mere coincidence; thus we fail to make a conscious effort to exercise our *innate ability* to intuitively perceive that which exists beyond the scope of the five senses. This innate ability then remains inactive; or at least *seemingly* inactive, obscured from regular awareness.

In addition to this; within the western hemisphere ... or at least western culture ... whether through schooling, upbringing, or societal "norms," many of us are primarily taught—and therefore more inclined—to utilise the logical faculties of the brain over the intuitive.

We are also somewhat encouraged to give stronger consideration to the tangible aspects of reality (i.e. physical forms) over the intangible aspects (i.e. thought *forms*) and so on.

As a result, what we perceive through the five senses usually stimulates a logical response, as we are inclined to make *logical sense* of what we see, hear, taste, touch and smell; commonly disregarding anything outside of these basic channels of awareness as myth, or "hocus-pocus."

Many of us will only acknowledge the intangible reality, beyond the five senses, through religion and prayer. Thus, occurrences of higher perception—and such that cannot be rationalised as originating from one of the five senses—are usually attributed, solely, to the workings of an external source (god, angels, the supernatural, and so on). Consequently, we overlook *our own inherent and natural abilities* to utilise this vast resource of power, of which we are a part.

Due to this lack of awareness, many people will even frown at, the mentioning alone of, some of the other disciplines (apart from prayer) that stimulate what is now known as extrasensory perception; practices such as: meditation, visualisation, chanting, breathing exercises, fasting, and so forth.

However, in the information-age mankind is certainly beginning to utilise more of this extrasensory ability, and the general awareness of such throughout the populace is consistently on the rise. Many new age scientists' and quantum physicists' are constantly verifying that extrasensory perception, and the ability to utilise it, is indeed *very real.*

This is also why there appear to be many phenomena—many mega structures—of the ancient world that still baffle us today; almost as though those who built them had some kind of "super-human abilities." Clearly they utilised faculties of the human brain (and mind) to a fuller degree.

To further add to my point here concerning the brain's unutilised potential, I would like to turn your attention toward a quote from the now late, but still renowned, self help author, Napoleon Hill.

Within a chapter entitled, *The Brain*; Hill brilliantly addressed this in the blockbusting international bestseller, *Think and Grow Rich* (23)*, originally written in 1937. And he did so within the section sub headed: *The Dramatic Story of the Brain.* And I quote:

"Last but not least, man, with all his boasted culture and education, understands little or nothing of the intangible force (the greatest of all intangibles) of thought. He knows but little concerning the physical brain, and its vast network of intricate machinery through which the power of thought is translated into its material equivalent, but he is now entering an age which shall yield enlightenment on the subject. Already men of science have begun to turn their attention to the study of this stupendous thing called the brain, and, while they are still in the kindergarten stage of their studies, they have uncovered enough

knowledge to know that the central switchboard of the human brain, the number of lines which connect the brain cells with one another, equal the figure one, followed by fifteen million ciphers."

Napoleon Hill then went on to quote, the also now late, Dr. C. Judson Herrick of the University of Chicago:

"*The figure is so stupendous that astronomical figures dealing with hundreds of millions of light years, become insignificant by comparison...It has been determined that there are from 10,000,000,000 to 14,000,000,000 nerve cells in the human cerebral cortex. And we know that these are arranged in definite patterns. These arrangements are not haphazard. They are orderly.*"

Hill, himself, then continued (and this is the key paragraph, concerning the brain, relevant to my point here): "*It is inconceivable that such a network of intricate machinery should be in existence for the sole purpose of carrying on the physical functions incidental to growth and maintenance of the human body. Is it not likely that the same system, which gives billions of brain cells the media for communication with one another, provides, also the means of communication with other intangible forces?*"

I would like to conclude this section on *the ten percent theory* by again stating that: *Yes*, while we may use more than 10 percent of the brain's *mass*, we do not necessarily use more than 10 percent of that mass's *full potential*.

The good news here is that with the right approach, knowhow, and level of awareness, we can indeed begin to utilise the dormant potential of the human brain. In essence much of what we call reality is based on various precepts and concepts. When we shift and expand these, we expand *Brain-potential*. We also expand our ability to utilise the Higher Mind potential of the universe as it relates to us.

So now that we have taken a quick look at the brain, how about the mind? Aren't the brain and the mind one and the same?

Mind

We use the mind every single day without fail, its presence so proverbial yet still so mystifying. Without the mind we are non-existent, yet with it we are eternal. However, if we are to truly utilise the mind to a greater degree; we must first have a basic understanding of some of its faculties.

If I were to casually mention the word "Mind," most people would think of the Brain. And although this could be seen as true; it would be largely dependent upon the individual's definition of "Mind."

As with the *Conscious Mind*, many biologists and scientists will attribute faculties of the *Subconscious Mind,* solely, to the— intricate and fascinating—workings of the human brain. On the other hand, many spiritualists tend to view these aspects of the mind as less tangible, even ethereal, in their existence.

But again, whether the many phenomena of the conscious and subconscious mind are said to be categorically attributed to the human brain, or not, is more so dependent upon the viewpoint of the person describing them.

Within the next section we will take a basic look at how some of the faculties which are typically associated with the mind correlate with known functions of the human brain. However, in favour of simplicity, I have not cited a great deal of technical terms for the many different areas of the brain while describing these faculties. Thus, throughout the majority of this chapter many of these "mind faculties" have been grouped under two simple terms: *the conscious mind* and *the subconscious mind.*

So, does this mean that the whole *Mind vs. Brain* argument is more a case of quibbling over semantics, than anything else? Well, not entirely. Although many of these faculties—which are commonly associated with the *conscious* and the *subconscious* mind—are actually attributable to the human brain; there is also what I refer to as the *Super-Conscious Mind* that we all have access to, *by way of the brain.* We will cover more on this later.

But first, in order for us to explore the mind a little further; the topic has been divided into three main categories, namely: *the subconscious mind, the conscious mind* and the *super-conscious mind.* And where you see the word "*consciousness*" used throughout this chapter, it is inclusive of all three categories and referring to Mind, as a whole. So without further ado, let's begin by taking a look at the...

Subconscious:

The subconscious mind, also referred to as the unconscious mind, is subjective as opposed to objective. *This means that it is not the area of the mind which deals with analysing, reasoning, rationale, logic and willpower;* but rather, *intuition, emotion, imagination, creativity and involuntary actions.*

As we covered within the foregoing section: *many traits of the subconscious mind do correspond, on a biological level, to relatively well known functions of the human brain.* The area of the brain commonly thought to be responsible for many of our subconscious faculties, is sometimes called: *The Old Brain.*

Judging by its name, "The Old Brain" (comprised mainly of what is sometimes referred to as "the reptilian brain," and the limbic system), it would appear somewhat obvious that this is the oldest domain within the structure of the human brain. In fact, it has been said (24) that this part of the brain began to evolve when amphibians crawled onto land and gave rise to the "reptilian age," and it remains fundamentally structured within the anatomy of the human brain to this day.

Therefore, this area of the brain is considerably ripened. It has developed and evolved throughout many hundreds of millions of years, right the way throughout our most primitive humanoid forms, up to date. It is that which our species utilised long before fluent forms of verbal linguistic communication and, hence, this part of the brain deals primarily with *emotion, intuition, creativity, involuntary actions, instinctual behaviour and so on.*

And as the Old Brain is the instinctive brain, it accounts for up to 95 percent of our day-to-day unconscious behavioural patterns. So if we are to effect real and lasting transformation within our lives, we must first learn to positively influence the subconscious elements of the mind (insofar as their relation to the Old Brain). Nonetheless, by utilising a number of the techniques, as suggested, throughout this book; you have already been doing just that.

Overall, the subconscious mind is extremely powerful but in order for us to utilise it more effectively we must first become well versed in its language: which is (besides emotions) the language of pictures and symbols: hence the importance of constructive visualisation.

It has been said that *a picture paints a thousand words*; which is to say, the underlying message of a thousand words could be conveyed within a single picture. But as the subconscious can assimilate information on a far greater scale, that picture (one thousand words) is akin to just one word in the language of the subconscious. And thus, the *meaning* of ten thousand words (figuratively speaking) can be conveyed in just one pictorial sentence (sequence).

This is a far more superior form of language. Ponder that for a moment. All improvement within your life begins with the improvement of your mental pictures, particularly your self *image*. This is also why affirmations without *visualisation* often produce diminutive results.

Now, at this point I would also like to mention that although the term *subconscious mind* has thus far been used with reference to the Old Brain; aside from the essential role of *Neuromelanin* (which we'll cover in a future publication), there is yet another key element of the subconscious mind which is infrequently addressed, and that is the role of the *Solar Plexus*. The Solar Plexus—sometimes referred to as *The Abdominal Brain*—is pivotal to the functioning of the *Autonomic Nervous System* and this is what manages the body's *involuntary actions*.

Although they are frequently separated by compartmentalised type thinking; the Old Brain, the Solar Plexus and the Autonomic Nervous System are all to be considered key elements of the subconscious mind which is, among other things, the *feeling* (intuitive) mind, as opposed to the thinking (conscious) mind.

The Solar Plexus also plays a large part in the *emotional* aspects of the subconscious faculties. In fact, it has been said that the Solar Plexus, *located just above the navel*, is the reason why we experience strong emotional feelings within the *pit of the stomach*, and the same is true of what we commonly refer to as "gut feelings."

The foregoing qualities, and more, are what render the subconscious mind such a major factor when utilising higher states of consciousness and *perceiving more*; nonetheless, because many of us are typically unaware of its phenomenal magnitude of power, we do not utilise it as fully as we could otherwise.

In essence, the subconscious mind is the medium through which extrasensory perception is possible. Higher thought forms and vibrations of energy can be received (from the super-conscious mind), and then presented to conscious awareness through flashes of intuition, or sudden insights and inspirations which seemingly "arise from nowhere."

The Essential Power

Similar to the example of the phone call earlier: somebody that you haven't seen for *many years* suddenly crosses your mind;

later on that day, "by chance," you happen to see that person and in excitement you say: "I was just thinking about you earlier", but after the initial surprise you both then disregard it as mere "coincidence."

But *no*, what if it's not *always* merely a coincidence. Instead, consider the possibility that this is a higher form of intuition at work; a higher form of intelligence that can be exercised and utilised to great effect once we acknowledge and embrace it.

However, typically because we cannot *logically* ("2 + 2 = 4" type thinking) explain it, we disregard it. And by doing so, we also disregard a significant portion of our intrinsic power by undermining this function of the *subconscious mind.* As a result we develop an imbalance between our use of the conscious (logical) and subconscious (intuitive) perceptive faculties.

Others might refer to this imbalance between the conscious and subconscious mind as an imbalance between the left and right brain hemispheres; logic and creativity; rigidified structure and total self expression; the outer adult and the inner child, etc. In essence the terms are inconsequential because the point remains the same. When we learn to better-utilise our subconscious we can bring about greater balance between its faculties and those of the conscious mind, we develop greater rapport between the two and as a result we *perceive more.*

When we effectively merge these qualities we enter the realm of "genii," but if not we stay relatively unaware of *the essential power* of the subconscious, consequently attributing much of its perceptive phenomena to various *external* sources (god, angels, spirits, the supernatural, and so forth).

However, in actuality there are no "external sources" because as we covered earlier, *everything is one*: interconnected in the form of energy. Therefore, the power outside is a reflection of the power inside and vice versa: "*as above, so below.*" A proverb merely echoed from the profound wisdom of the sagacious throughout many ancient cultures.

Far Greater Abilities

With this understanding, it is no surprise that a number of our predecessors—responsible for engineering many *wonders* of the ancient world—managed to accomplish great feats: many of which, modern thinking (which is frequently dependent upon the *logical* faculties, primarily encouraged throughout the western educational system) still cannot comprehend or replicate to this day.

The level of technology involved in the masonry of many of the *ancient* structures worldwide (pyramids, temples, stone carvings etc.) is a plain and unarguable testament of this. In this regard, the architects and builders of that time clearly utilised faculties of the mind above and beyond that which we, as their descendents, typically do today.

Despite the proletarian depiction of slaves with primitive tools—which is propagated by a number of mainstream Egyptologists and historians to this day—just a little *objective* research into this field will confirm that these ancient builders clearly utilised a superior degree of consciousness. This is evidenced by their far-advanced feats of masonry, architecture, precision, geometry, symbolism, geology and magnetism (to name a few).

The learned of that day and time had an advanced understanding of mind power. They achieved a greater degree of balance between the conscious, subconscious and super-conscious mind (varying degrees of the same source); with the result being an advanced state of *consciousness*, clearly evident in their architecture; particularly the great pyramid of Giza, Egypt, *Africa!*

Not only was there a focus on developing the faculties of the conscious mind, but they also dedicated much interest toward developing and utilising the faculties of the *subconscious* (intuitive/creative) mind; thereby heightening the ability to tune in with *super-consciousness* more freely.

By contrast, nowadays, particularly within western culture, there is very little focus on the significance of these two latter *key elements* of mind power. Thus we experience a limited paradigm, primarily through the *conscious* (logical/analytical) mind.

This is the paradigm which is most highly valued throughout today's society, and this is not only evident throughout the educational system, but also as a basic methodology within mainstream scientific research—which is primarily based upon that which can be *rationalised* and *reasoned* (both being foremost functions of the conscious mind) or at the very least hypothesised.

This global shift in consciousness, from then to now, brings yet another meaning to the phrase *"from one 'state of mind' to another."*

However, we can *truly* begin to *perceive more* by acknowledging and utilising the faculties of the *conscious, subconscious* and the *super-conscious* mind, collectively. And therefore, the chief aim of the information within this chapter is to bring awareness to some of their *basic* functions for this very purpose.

Many of the achievements of the ancients—along with their advanced knowledge of the celestial bodies—merely seem unexplainable to us because, nowadays, many of us are not utilising our subconscious faculties as fully as we could.

Nonetheless, we have the capacity to unlock this dormant potential. Everything being stated here: you already know. It is all innately stored within your subconscious mind. This is merely a re-*mind*-er.

We all have *far greater abilities* than we are generally taught to acknowledge, or utilise, throughout conventional forms of education. And with the correct approach and knowhow we can begin to awaken these great, but often dormant, qualities.

As touched upon within the opening section; we are all connected to an *Infinitely Vast Creative Intelligence: Universal Mind* (or whatever name you want to give it). And therefore we intrinsically share its attributes with the only differences being merely those of degree.

Now that we've gained a small insight into the power and magnitude of the subconscious mind as it relates to the greater scheme of things, let's now turn our attention toward some of its basic everyday functions; one of which being the maintenance of the involuntary actions within the body.

Involuntary Actions

By use of the word *involuntary* I am referring to the actions within the body that are carried out independent of one's will.

A few pages back we touched upon the fact that the subconscious mind is *not* responsible for the faculties of willpower or conscious reasoning; however, this inability of the subconscious mind—to reason things out—is not to be considered a weakness. In fact, it is quintessential to its power. And one reason for this is simply because the subconscious mind is also responsible for the involuntary actions of the body.

Imagine if our subconscious had to *reason out* and decide whether all the cells (apart from the blood and reproductive cells) within our body should continue to manufacture their 2000 proteins per second: or whether the 100 trillion cells within an adult person's body should produce protein chains that flawlessly organize some 150,000,000,000,000,000,000 (150 quintillion) amino acids every hour.

To add to this, imagine the subconscious had to *reason out* whether our white blood cells should subject another 10 billion cells in our body to health checks every 2 seconds: or to keep it simple, just imagine that you had to *reason out* whether your heart should continue to pump blood around the body. It is nothing short of a marvel that all of this—and more—is taken care of on "autopilot," by way of the subconscious mind.

However; in addition to the involuntary actions of the body, the mind also has one of its own which I like to call *the little chatterbox.* By this I am referring to the (largely unconscious) unremitting stream of thoughts that pass through our minds every day.

Little Chatterbox

While it is true that we can consciously direct our thinking, it is also true that many of our thoughts arise involuntarily.

If you disagree with the above statement then I challenge you to briefly put this book down, right now, and attempt to stop all thoughts from entering your mind for just two minutes. This does not mean to day dream, nor does it mean to hold your attention on a single thought, but to absolutely clear the mind of *all* thought: pure nothingness. You will soon realise how thoughts can often pop up, involuntarily.

We all have internal dialogue with ourselves. Sometimes this self-talk is conscious and other times unconscious, but either way we all have a *little chatterbox* which constantly opinionates and judges things that we experience.

It's possible that at this point you might even be thinking "I don't have a little chatterbox: what little chatterbox?" *That one!*

When this internal "little voice" is of an *empowering* nature, and we spontaneously act upon it, great things are often accomplished. But on the other hand, if it is one of cynicism and self-doubt then we severely limit our self-expression and potential by becoming unconsciously identified with it.

If many of the thoughts that arise within your mind are negative (such as thoughts of doubt, cynicism, deceit, spite, vengefulness, slander, violence, etc.) then you must first realise that your subconscious mind is only spewing back out whatever you have been allowing in. It is merely playing back to you (by way of electrical impulses and chemical reactions within the brain) whatever it has been *fed* over a period of time.

Stop feeding your mind thoughts of doubt, worry, guilt and negativity; and it will stop vomiting them up in the face of opportunity. Limit the tendency to be entertained by— seemingly harmless—negative influences (soap-operas, newspaper articles, negative music, negative people, etc.) or at least balance them out with positive ones.

What are you allowing into your mind on a daily basis? Whatever you put in, is what you get out. The corresponding law of nature is universal: *You reap what you sow.*

Just imagine a farmer expecting a generous harvest of crops in the growing season, without first planting any seeds. Furthermore, imagine that same farmer planting corn seeds but expecting a harvest of wheat crops? "How ridiculous" you might correctly say; overlooking the fact that many of us *mindlessly* follow the same pattern.

We desire the harvest of a more positive and confident mindset, yet we continually sow the seeds of negativity and self-doubt; worst still, we allow others to sow them for us.

If you are constantly entertaining (sowing) the seeds of negative stimuli, then much of your unconscious internal dialogue will reflect that: reaping the thoughts of a corresponding nature. However, *this will also happen vice versa with constructive influences and thoughts which are translated into a mindset of empowerment.*

Many people will say that the subconscious mind manifests our thoughts into reality, but they do so while simultaneously overlooking the most common process by which this occurs. *The subconscious mind manifests our thoughts into reality because we are typically inclined to "unconsciously" act upon many of the thoughts that our "little chatterbox" is spewing out: based on what it has been fed.*

If you fully comprehend the significance of the preceding sentence you will immediately grasp the importance of replacing negative *habitual* thinking patterns, with those of empowerment.

As human beings, we are generally "creatures of habit," and all habits start within the mind as a result of our thinking patterns. Habits become such, when they have been embedded within the subconscious mind over a period of time through repetition, whether consciously or unconsciously.

Replacing our disempowering habits with those of empowerment and, thereby, maintaining an optimistic attitude and internal dialogue is the *aim of the game*. And to master this "game" it requires skill like any other. It requires perseverance and dedicated consistent practice, but once this skill is mastered it becomes forever stored within the subconscious mind, which plays a key role in acquiring any skill set.

Learning a Skill

The brain has billions of neurons that connect at trillions of points. These neurons send signals between one other by electrical impulses. When certain neurons send large numbers of electrical impulses to other neurons, this activity can be measured in the form of waves: we call these *brain waves*. When we are learning a skill ... any skill ... for the first time; we are creating new neurological pathways (connections between neurons) within the brain. And thus, these pathways between the associated neurons become stronger every time that we repeat the action ("practice makes perfect").

The information is then stored within the subconscious mind (responsible for long term memory), and once this happens we are able to perform this skill without *consciously focusing* as hard as we had to initially; therefore it becomes more "natural." And this is true whether it's a purely mental task regarding our thought habits (i.e. replacing negative ways of thinking with empowering thought patterns) or indeed a physical task (i.e. riding a bicycle).

Furthermore, do you remember when you first learnt to ride a bicycle; and you had to be as *alert* as possible, keenly *focusing* on every little movement? Well, at that moment you were predominantly employing the faculties of your *conscious* mind (focus, concentration, awareness, logic, reason, etc.).

But after a little repetition, your neurological connections for "bike riding" became stronger, and thus your level of skill increased in this area. You could now ride the bicycle more "naturally," without having to *concentrate* as hard as you did when initially learning.

Your increased ability to perform that skill without excessive concentration was because the "bike riding information" was now pre-stored within the *subconscious mind*; ready to be employed at any given time. You could then achieve the same results but with less concentration, and thus you could direct some of your *conscious attention* toward something else i.e., having a conversation while you were riding.

Whatever task you are engaged in at any given moment, you are physically modifying your brain to become better at it. This is because whenever we are doing (or thinking) something; the neurological pathways in the brain (for this action or thought) are strengthened, thus reinforcing the impression upon the subconscious mind.

So the question is: what are you modifying your brain to become better at the majority of the time? Are they activities of empowerment that will uplift you, or those of disempowerment that will eventually weaken you? This is a two part question worth answering.

The Principle of Association

Aside from learning a skill, the subconscious mind could also be likened to a giant warehouse which encompasses our past memories. Information which is experienced through the senses is then stored within the *subconscious* for future reference, and we are continuously drawing upon this data in order for us to evaluate new experiences.

For example, when meeting someone for the first time we consciously observe details about them: what they look like, how they dress, certain characteristics, personality traits and so forth. Our conscious mind then rapidly delivers this information to our subconscious mind looking for references (memories), with which we can compare and evaluate the new data.

In other words we evaluate people, places and things based on the information of past knowledge and experiences that we believe to be true. Of course, this is fairly simple to comprehend, but this can also influence our decisions unconsciously, that is to say, without us being *aware* of it.

For example: most of us have probably experienced a situation at some point, where we took a genuine liking to a total stranger, without knowing why. "I don't know what it is about that person, but there's just something about them" we might have thought to ourselves. Admittedly there could be varying factors for this but one such factor could be that this person, say, "Jenny," might appear similar—in some respects—to someone that we got along with in our distant past somewhere, "Jane."

Now, because we got on with Jane naturally an association was made: we associated a *positive emotional state* with Jane's type of appearance. And although we can't remember Jane, per se (perhaps even from early childhood), our subconscious mind, which is responsible for long term-memory, still has this equation stored.

This feeling is then triggered and brought forward when we meet "Jenny," who even though is a total stranger, bears some sort of similarity to Jane: causing us to be instantly more receptive to this type of appearance. Of course this can also happen consciously too, as in "You remind me of this or that person."

In terms of memory, the subconscious mind works on the principle of association and uses information that we have gathered throughout our lifetime accordingly.

It then attempts to manifest (through conscious awareness) certain situations into our lives which are in alignment with our most dominant thoughts and memories. And this is especially true of thoughts that have been keenly mixed with emotion and expectancy.

An Excellent Goal Achieving Agency

For this reason the subconscious is an excellent goal achieving agency because your most dominant thoughts are guaranteed to manifest. Master your most dominant thoughts and by default you will master your destiny. But take note; this is an entirely neutral process.

The subconscious mind will just as readily manifest dominant thoughts of negativity, as it will those of positivity. And this is because you will naturally—often without realising it—be attracted to the persons, places and things which are in sync with those thoughts, and when you are, thus they manifest.

It is this fact which accounts for the huge importance of becoming more aware of which thoughts you choose to entertain and become emotionally invested with. Those of positivity and productivity will lead to you attaining your desired goals, while those of doubt and indifference will do exactly the opposite.

It's a shame that so many people entertain this latter variety, while simultaneously wondering why they are not excelling at a steady pace throughout life. Remember, thought forms *always* precede physical forms. Think productive (consistently), and your environment will become a product of your productivity.

The Conscious Mind:

In contrast to the "Old Brain" (located at the inner areas and base of the entire brain) that we spoke of earlier; the *New Brain* (as in, the later developed areas of the human brain) is thought by some to have evolved within the "higher mammals" reaching its zenith within humans. The "New Brain" is also indescribably essential and extremely powerful. It is the epitome of conscious *human* perception. And it is comprised mainly of the two hemispheres of the Neocortex (the outer areas of the brain).

Many functions of the New Brain correspond with a number of faculties which are typically associated with the *conscious* mind. These regions are thus thought to be primarily responsible for: *logic, attentiveness, reasoning, rationale, verbal language and so on.*

The Conscious Mind is also sometimes referred to as the *objective mind*, and it is that which governs the overall ability of *awareness.* You are consciously aware anytime that you are: exercising your willpower; pondering or concentrating; analysing or rationalising; comparing or criticising; accepting or rejecting information; reaching logical conclusions and so forth. In short, you are *conscious* anytime that you are *aware*.

This is of great significance as far as humans are concerned because we are typically considered to be the most intelligent species of the animal kingdom; and this is chiefly due to our superior capacity to exercise *self awareness* and *conscious reasoning*, enabling us to study our own behaviour and make logical decisions between complex choices. We are then able to exercise our willpower and take action based on those decisions.

Aside from the phenomenal power of concentration and the mighty force of willpower, *self-awareness* along with the capacity to *reason* things out is why the conscious mind has such a vital role. Because it is by way of these qualities that we are able to consciously decipher, filter out, and influence, many of the programmes that will be stored within the subconscious mind for later reference.

It is also through the conscious mind that we form a sense of personal identity which in turn gives rise to the ego. However, although it may be a bitter pill to swallow, the stark truth is that your identity—as in, how you perceive yourself to be—is very much a *conceptual construct* which is maintained by the logical aspect of your conscious mind, in order to provide a sense of identity and meaning.

This is important because our *image of self,* our identity, often provides the frame of reference from which we view the world, therefore our perception of the external world is biased by how we see ourselves in relation to it. To put it simply, we see the world as *we* are; mentally filtering experiences until they are consistent with the distinguished context of our own *identity.* And the rigidity of these boundaries, created by the conscious mind, then determine the degree to which we can become truly self aware.

In addition to this, the conscious mind is also intimately connected to our ability to memorise; as oftentimes we cannot remember something if we were not paying *attention* when it happened. In this regard, the strength of the attention can determine the depth of the memory.

Identified & Accepted

As the subconscious mind is the realm of the emotions, an emotional experience creates a stronger impression upon it. Thus when we strongly identify with something, whether positive or negative, that information is then more readily used as a point of reference with which the *conscious mind* will compare new experiences in the future.

However, the subconscious is less likely to present these—to conscious awareness—as dominant memories or ideas if we were less identified and emotionally invested at the time they were formed. For example; if somebody calls me "useless," and I *consciously* choose to become emotionally identified with their insult, then that experience is likely to create a deeper impression upon my subconscious mind and will thus become a internal reference for any subsequent criticism (remember, we spoke about references in the chapter: *Limiting Beliefs*).

On the other hand if I choose *not* to emotionally identify with their insult but, instead, to consciously reject it; then it's less likely to be the first thing to mind if I'm criticised at a later date, and therefore I would be less limited by it.

The Sentinel

As we saw earlier, the conscious mind is responsible for accepting or rejecting information because the subconscious is subjective in nature. In this regard the conscious mind could be seen as *the sentinel.* But due to many of us being oblivious of this "sentinel" type duty of the conscious mind, sometimes we may allow disempowering messages to slip through the "unguarded gate" and on into the subconscious storehouse for later reference.

Once we identify with an idea or accept it as fact; this "fact" will often begin to *unconsciously* influence any subsequent decisions that we make in relation to it: i.e., if it were a *fact*, to you, that you'd succeed in all that you done, you'd probably make a *decision* to do more things; and the same applies vice versa. However, both of these are dependent upon what you're focusing on (with, *focus,* being a foremost faculty of the *conscious mind*). When necessary, the ability to keenly *focus* and *concentrate* on a single idea is a mighty force which can be used to deeply impress an idea upon the subconscious mind.

Concentration directs the energies of the conscious mind to a focal point, similar to how light can be *concentrated* into a laser beam. It is a quality of indispensable magnitude and one well worth developing and strengthening, providing we know when best to utilise it.

Concentration brings the smaller details into focus; it is like the magnifying glass, and you can either magnify thoughts of empowerment or you can magnify those of doubt and worry. Nonetheless, one possible way of lessening the tendency to indulge in the latter, is by exercising what I like to call: *Context-Intelligence;* or, CI.

Becoming Context-Intelligent

The ability to see things from different contexts is a function of the conscious mind made possible through our ability to reason. Reasoning is often dependent upon our capacity to identify, compare and evaluate different contexts; or put simply, ways of looking at things. This is what I refer to as context-intelligence.

For our purpose here, by use of the word *context* I am referring to an individual's reference frame, as in, their perception or viewpoint toward an experience.

Any experience can have different shades of meaning, which need to be interpreted by the context. The context determines the meaning that we attach to an experience which, in turn, influences how we respond. Change the context and a "problem" becomes an opportunity; a failure becomes a valuable stepping stone; a perceived weakness (fear) becomes a temporary source of power.

The context in which we view something determines the point of view that we see it from, and each time we shift our point of view, our reference frame, we gain access into new realms of perceiving that were unavailable from the preceding isolated viewpoint.

Why is this important? It's important because a person's ability to view things from different contexts determines the range of their *conscious awareness*. And a greater range of awareness enables us to perceive things which others cannot. As a result we become less limited in our responses and able to utilise a wider scope of self-expression. We perceive that which is beyond the *content* by being able to shift the *context*.

In this case, the content represents the details of an experience, but the context represents how we view it and, thus, what we make it *mean* to us. *Content* intelligence demonstrates knowledge, but *context* intelligence demonstrates wisdom.

If we confine ourselves to viewing things from a set and rigid paradigm then, by default, we become one-dimensional. But with the ability to shift between different frames of reference we become multi-dimensional in our awareness. *We begin perceiving more*. In a sense our CI is the true measure of our conscious intelligence; nonetheless, neither of these can be accurately calculated by way of the standard "Intelligence Quotient" (IQ) test.

The IQ Test and the Measure of Intelligence

It is sometimes thought possible to gauge an individual's level of intelligence by such means as an IQ test. However, the one-size-fits-all methodology of an IQ test is a fundamentally flawed concept because it does not take into account many of the complexities of cognitive processing.

A person's true intellectual ability cannot be epitomised by an IQ test because along with other factors, intellectual ability is dependent upon short term memory, *conscious reasoning* and verbal agility. And although they work synergistically, these faculties are the functions of three distinct nerve centres within the brain. An individual may be acute in one of these areas, but this does not necessarily exhibit their strength within the other two.

In addition to this; cultural elements also come into play when demonstrating the erroneous authority of IQ tests. As cultural identity is one of the primary frames of reference for an individual, an IQ test that has been designed biased to a particular culture cannot then be used to accurately gauge the general intelligence of those foreign to that cultural experience.

And this is moreover dependent upon which facet of intelligence that particular culture tends to value the most i.e., logical intelligence, creative intelligence, social intelligence and so forth. From this perspective, even the phrase "culture free intelligence test" is a contradiction in terms.

But even aside from the cultural element; a number of additional factors can also influence the results of an IQ test. These are things such as: sleep deprivation; a person's mood at the time of the test; their background experiences; their social experience; their immediate concerns; their environment; their perception; their learning style; their CI, their Map; and the list goes on.

Therefore, on a wider scale, general intelligence could be seen as the measure of an individual's ability to perceive, interpret, learn from, understand, and interact with themselves, others, and their environment. And although this is the result of both intricate and complex faculties of cognitive processing; overall it is the conscious mind, through the power of *reasoning* and *context intelligence,* which is quintessential to this ability.

Body-Part Context

People with a high degree of CI are able to identify and utilise different frames of reference, they can voluntarily change the lenses through which they view an experience; and even study the lenses themselves. They are not rigidly bound within a set way of perceiving. To put it simply, *they perceive more.*

And this is simply because when viewing something from a certain context; it allows us to then see the different possibilities which are consistent with that context. To further illustrate this, take your open hand and lay it palm down on your lap, tuck your fingers to make a fist then point only your index outward. Now take a moment to keenly observe it and then say, out loud, what you see.

Most people would say that they see a finger; others might describe it in more detail noticing the knuckle, the lines going across the finger, the nail, the cuticle of the nail and so forth.

Others may be more analytical still, noticing the texture, the fine hairs and tiny hair follicles. And although this description would be correct, it is focused solely on the content. It would not signify *context* intelligence because it is one dimensionally limited to the context of *body part*, as in, the finger itself.

But now look at your finger again from the context of numbers, what number do you see? Now again from the context of colour, what colours do you see? How about from the context of direction, as if you were pointing at something? Finally, what do you see from the context of shapes?

By now you would have noticed that although your finger has not physically changed in anyway, it can signify different meanings dependent on the context. And by simply changing the context from body part (finger) to numbers or colours, direction or shapes; you then, respectively, became *consciously aware* of all the possibilities consistent with each realm.

When I first asked what you saw and you said "a finger," the number one was always there as a possibility, as was the colour, the direction, the shape and so forth, but you were oblivious to those contextual distinctions because your awareness was fixed within the context of body part.

Just think; what opportunities or possibilities are you overlooking in your life right now because you have become accustomed to the view of a fixed context?

Right now within your life there are opportunities and possibilities that are as obvious as the number one was with your finger, but without utilising your CI you will remain unaware of them. As the great poet Rumi, once said: *"When we change the way we look at things, the things we look at change."*

Now that we have taken a look at a few of the faculties of the subconscious and the conscious mind, I would like to turn your attention toward...

Super-Consciousness:

The super-conscious mind exists not as a *place* of existence but, more so, a *plane* of existence. It is that which is nearer in vibratory state to the *Universal Mind*: essentially they are the same source with the only distinction being one of degree.

The super-conscious element of the mind is the only aspect of this phenomenal resource which cannot *solely* be attributed to the workings of the brain.

Moreover; it is this super-conscious mind that we are all attuned to, *by way of the brain,* which makes certain "phenomena" (i.e. morphic resonance, global consciousness, telepathy, remote viewing, déjà vu, and many others) possible.

The Antenna

To put it simply, *the super-conscious mind* could be likened to a "vibrational frequency" for which the brain is a "transceiver." (By use of the word "Brain" I am also referring to the entire nervous system, which is simply an extension of the brain within the skull. The nervous system can be further divided into sub-systems; nonetheless all of these are still composed of *neurons* and connective tissue.)

Similar to how a television receives the signal from a satellite, via its antenna; the human brain can also transmit, and receive, "signals" to, and from, the vibrational field of super-consciousness. Invisible information is all around us; even right now, as you are reading these words, there is electromagnetic radiation passing through your body. And this electromagnetic energy is how we send wireless messages around the globe at lightning speeds.

In an era of wireless communication we transmit information in various energy waves. Whether they are radio waves, television waves, microwaves, and so on, they are all man-utilised forms of electromagnetic energy; and this energy is passing through many of us all day, every day: whether it's from the mobile phone, the computer, the radio, or any other wireless device for that matter. These types of EM waves are, of course, measurable with modern scientific equipment and that is how we manipulate and utilise them to our benefit.

The point here is simply to re-emphasise the fact that there is information (invisible to the naked eye) being transmitted around, and through, us constantly. The information of someone's mobile telephone conversation could be passing through you at this very moment in the form of electromagnetic energy.

From this *viewpoint*, we hardly require a leap of faith to accept that what appears to be the empty space between you and this book; is not empty at all. In fact, it is *far* from it. There is a great deal of *information* being transmitted through this "empty space" which is undetected by the five senses.

Although some forms of energy (i.e. electromagnetic); can be easily measured with the right equipment; there are still other types of energy that cannot be, and *super-consciousness* "falls" into the latter. However, as the most advanced computer known to man, the human brain can pick up information from various sources of energy, ranging from super-consciousness right through to radio waves.

Just think: in regards to the latter, have you ever thought of a song and then switched on your radio and that song was playing; or perhaps a similar thing happened with a television programme? You thought that it was merely a coincidence right?

Perhaps it was. But on the other hand, consider the possibility that *your brain* (acting as an "antenna") momentarily received and interpreted, the same information that was being transmitted in the form of radio waves (through what you thought was empty space) to your television or radio.

It is also in a similar fashion that the human brain can receive, transmit, and interpret information from *super-consciousness,* and it does so by way of the *subconscious mind,* which then presents this information to conscious awareness, via the conscious mind.

We all have unlimited access to a great deal of energy, information and creativity within any given moment. It literally permeates all that exists. Therefore higher states of consciousness are *always* accessible, but we must tune in to them. And this can be facilitated by the use of certain herbs and/or the employment of various practices such as: meditation, visualisation, rhythmic breathing, chanting, yoga, correct diet and various others.

If we choose to acknowledge and trust it, the super-conscious mind can indeed be utilised to an infinite extent. And we *all* have the capacity to access this ability in varying degrees, dependent upon our state of *consciousness* at the time.

Feeding the Mind:

Although I maintain the opinion that Meditation is the one practice which has the *ultimate* benefit for the mind; we will not divulge here into matters considered to be, more so, *spiritual* in nature. That will be a later publication. But for now we will focus on some simple ideas for influencing the mind— particularly the subconscious mind—that can be used at any time.

When it comes to feeding the *subconscious mind*, as mentioned earlier, it is indiscriminate. If we are constantly feeding it with negative thoughts such as: *"Things always go wrong for me," "I'll never be able to achieve this or that;" "I always have bad luck*," and so forth; then we need not be surprised when the corresponding results manifest as our reality.

Positive Affirmations

The good news is that we can begin to change this for the better at any time. In order to do so, one method that we can use requires a little persistence on our part, and it involves the consistent repetition of positive and empowering thoughts on a regular basis; thereby creating new neurological pathways within the brain.

In much the same way that we would consistently repeat an action in order for it to become a skill, or habit; the same principle applies to the type of thoughts that we think, which then determine our actions.

Transforming some of our innermost thought patterns is what will facilitate real and lasting change within our lives. And by now it should be clear that one way to impress something—that you want to achieve—upon the subconscious mind is by sheer repetition: in this case the repetition of certain affirmations.

However; constantly repeating just the bland words of an affirmation alone, will not produce great results. But as we saw earlier, for maximum effectiveness, it's just as important that the words of the affirmation are emotionalised and fully identified with.

We could then substitute those old limiting beliefs with affirmations such as: "*I can achieve anything that I put my mind to*," "*I have massive potential*," "*Any challenge is simply an opportunity for me to become an even stronger person*," "*When*

*one door closes another two doors open" "I don't focus on the
door that closes for so long, that I miss the two that open,"
"There is an opportunity in every setback," "I am strong" "I am
powerful," and so on* (there are more of these at the back of this
book).

*Repeated positive affirmations are the continuous optimistic
assertions, in the present tense, of any attributes or conditions
that we wish to strengthen or instigate.* All of us can positively
influence our subconscious mind in order for us to bring about
better results within our lives, and we can do this by consistently
feeding it nourishing, uplifting, well emotionalised thoughts;
with repetition, faith and expectancy.

While affirming something, it will significantly boost your
results if you feel the corresponding emotion to the affirmation;
this is what I have been referring to as "emotionalised thought."
For example, if you are affirming "I am strong and confident"
then don't just sit there with your head held low and shoulders
shrugged forward; visualise yourself as being assertive, get
yourself into a state of confidence (see: *posture*, page 137).

Remember, the subconscious is also the realm of the emotions,
so go ahead and conjure up the corresponding emotion to what it
is that you are affirming, or wanting to achieve. And vividly
visualise yourself as having already accomplished it; this way
you will then be guaranteed far greater results than just
repeatedly stating the bland words alone.

At the back of this book, I have included a number of one-liner
affirmations, corresponding with the order of the chapters
throughout. I have also included a complete version of one of

the actual affirmations, among many, which I still use now: tailor it how you please, more importantly, *get started*. But before you do, here are the key points to remember:

1. Affirmations need to be repeated regularly and consistently over a period of time. The more often the repetition, the deeper the groove within the subconscious mind; and the more natural the desired trait becomes (remember; learning a skill). Unwavering repetition may sometimes occur tiresome, but remember to steadfast, *"progress is a process"* (see chapter 3: *Steadfast*).

2. One word; *expectancy!* With affirmations, the results which you achieve will be directly in line with your faith in their ability to work. Keenly *expect* them to work, even before you start.

3. Always state an affirmation in the present tense. Not *"I am going to,"* or *"I will do,"* but instead *"I do...,"* *"I am...,"* *"I have...,"* and so forth.

4. Preferably, affirmations should be stated in the "positive" and not the "negative;" i.e. *"I am powerful"* as opposed to, *"I am not weak."* Use *"I am's"* instead of *"I am not's."*

5. KEY POINT: For maximum results, affirmations should not only be consistently and regularly repeated, in the present tense, (until you achieve the desired results) but they also should, *always,* be accompanied with the vivid visualisation, and keen emotion, of that which you are affirming.

If the affirmation is not ardently emotionalised and envisioned you may be doing yourself a great disservice. Remember, you want to make a deep and lasting impact within the subconscious mind (at the root) in order for these affirmations to be noticeably effective. It is the subconscious (underlying) faculties that must be "rewired" in order to gain a deep rooted foundation for long term results.

Some people experience great results when using affirmations, and others, not so great. However, sometimes this can be more so the result of the individual's method of approach; and also how *identified* they can become (by applying point 5) with what they are affirming.

As earlier mentioned in point 2, when *affirming*, the results which you achieve will be directly in alignment, with your faith in their ability to work (which will also increase with each result). Believe that they will and they will, believe that they won't and you need not be surprised when they don't. If you have used affirmations before and they have not worked for you, it may have been due to this reason.

You could first begin to remedy this by using an affirmation on itself. Do this by first impressing upon your subconscious mind that they work without doubt, i.e., *"Affirmations are powerful because whatever I sincerely repeat to my subconscious mind becomes my reality."*

Personally, I have experienced noticeable results when using affirmations, and this is because I unwaveringly expect them to be effective. Either way, although they can help, affirmations are not "the silver bullet,"— no *one* technique is.

Nonetheless, they can be a good place to start; used alone, or in unison with many of the other techniques found throughout this book. But the main key here is not just using affirmations, but also to take some bold new action. *Experience is the best teacher.*

Following on from this, the type of language that we use also plays an essential role in how we perceive things.

Using Empowering Language

Language is a crucial element of *perceiving more*. It is one of the fundamental means by which our minds make sense of things. As we touched upon within the chapter on *Steadfast*, (see page 62) the scope of language that we use on a daily basis has an essential role in shaping our reality and thus it can broaden it, or limit it.

Make a small commitment to learn at least one new word every day. If you have access to the internet, you could simply type in the phrase "word of the day" into your web browser. You will then be presented with a number of different websites that upload a different word every day, along with its meaning.

Select a website, and then each day simply endeavour to fit their "word of the day" into your vocabulary as many times as you can throughout that day. The more that you use it, the more you will remember it.

Needless to say; after just one month, that's thirty (or so) new words and therefore, thirty new possible ways of expressing yourself verbally. Remember the *"penny or a million £s"* question back in the chapter on *Steadfast*? The little things can indeed "add up" over time and begin to make huge differences.

Broadening our vocabulary can also help to broaden our perspective in general. This is because it enables us to specifically define things where we, perhaps, wouldn't have done before, as effectively.

As a shallow example of this; has there ever been something that you were attempting to communicate to someone, but you couldn't think of the right words to describe it? You probably wound up saying something like; "Oh, I can't explain it." And as a result the person that you were talking to couldn't fully grasp the importance of your point: such are boundaries of a limited vocabulary.

The words that we use can have an almost indescribable effect on how we perceive ourselves, and indeed the world at large. Words, within their spoken form, or thought form, are essentially one of the key components that shape our perception of reality. They have a hypnotic power that can greatly influence how we feel at any given time.

It has been said that; in certain cultures of ancient times those who were most literate (in terms of reading, writing and drawing) were seen as *mystics*. And this was because they had the ability to name and define (decipher) things; they were able to bring things into existence through the use of language.

Think about it; without some type of label or illustration to define the meaning of a thing—as far as language and depiction are concerned—that thing would be nonexistent.

For instance; what would you call the chair that you are sitting on right now if you didn't have a name for it? You wouldn't call it anything. It would have no linguistic definition. It would still be there, yet you would be unable to linguistically define the *meaning* of it.

Hence there were certain literates, of old, who were seen as mystics that could bring great *meaning* (through definition) to life. And in addition to this, they were highly revered for their ability to document sacred records that were to be preserved and passed down to future generations.

Just as the mystics of old, we too bring things into existence by our use of certain words and labels, along with meanings that we attach to them. For instance, the innocent, but hyperactive, child that can't seem to sit still or focus for long periods of time could be labelled as having an *Attention Deficit Hyperactivity Disorder (ADHD)*. The label then takes on a life of its own in accordance with the meaning attached to it, thus we have now brought a "disorder" into existence purely through the use of language.

When we first learn words we assign meaning to them based on interpretation, or by listening to the context in which they are used. The meanings (and feelings) that we attach to these words are then stored subconsciously and every time the word is used there is a subconscious (subtle emotional) pattern attached to it.

Although this is an entirely neutral process, the question here is: what reality are you creating for yourself with the words that you are using daily? A number of the forthcoming substitutes were inspired by Susan Jeffers within her brilliant book: *Feel the fear and do it anyway* (25).

Here are just a few shallow examples of how words can influence our reality by altering our perception. I would perhaps recommend substituting a number of the following:

I. "I'm going to try..." (implies failure, lack of confidence) – with – "I'm going to do..." (confidence, certainty, positivity)

II. "I Can't..." (no choice, failure) – with – "I Won't..." (implies choice, control)

III. "I Should..." (burden, pressure, guilt) – with – "I Could..." (again, this implies more choice, control)

IV. "It's a problem" (negative) – with – "It's a challenge" (an opportunity to learn and test my skills (positive))

V. "I'm never satisfied" (guilt) – with – "I continually want to learn and grow" (empowerment)

VI. "Life's a struggle" (barely coping) – with – "life's an adventure" (excitement, enthusiasm)

VII. "If only..." (uncertainty) – with – "Next time..." (certainty)

VIII. "What will I do?" (uncertainty, fear) – with – "I know I can handle it" (certainty, confidence)

IX. "I hope that..." (out of your control, uncertainty) – with – "I trust that..." (certainty)

Reframing

Reframing is the ability to change how we view something, by shifting the *meaning* of that thing. This simple technique can also be useful for influencing our emotional states because the meaning we give something, usually determines how we feel towards it.

Literally anything can be reframed because, as we covered earlier, what we perceive as reality is essentially a subjective experience via our *deletions, distortions* and *generalisations*. In reality, events themselves are entirely neutral, until we judge them; filtered through our values, beliefs, our morals and so on.

The meaning of an experience is dependent upon the context in which we view it. By reframing an experience, we then have a stronger platform from which we can control our emotional responses in the moment.

Imagine one of the pictures on your wall at home—assuming that you have any. If you were to only frame a tiny portion of that picture, would it have the same meaning? No, of course not! Similarly; would that picture look the same with a 24 carat gold frame, as it would with a cheaper plastic frame from our local Poundland Store? No, of course not!

A similar perspective could also be applied when reframing the context in which we view something. Reframing (giving another meaning to) a picture (an experience) can be useful; particularly when we are faced with adversity because we can then look at— what otherwise might have been seen as—a "problem" in a more empowering light.

For an example of this, John, a client of mine, once said to me; "When I get up to speak in front of my team at the office I know some people are mocking me because I can see them smiling." I thought about John's statement momentarily, and then to reframe this I replied "John, have you ever read something in a book, or magazine, that resonated with you so much that you momentarily smiled to yourself?" "Yes of course," he replied, with a bewildered expression, wondering what my point was.

I then continued; "When someone is giving a talk in front of the team at my office, I usually smile if I feel really inspired by something they said." John nodded his head *and smiled to himself* right there and then, in agreement.

Now when John gives presentations in front of his team at the office, if people tend to smile while he is presenting he no longer translates it as mockery but, instead, his ability to inspire people.

Whether this is *actually* the case or not really doesn't matter; what *does* matter is that John now has a considerably more empowering attitude toward his speaking. This will then boost his confidence and as a result, if he wasn't particularly inspiring before, with this heightened sense of confidence the chances are that he is now.

By reframing we can shift our perspective to view a problem as an opportunity; a weakness as a strength; an impossibility as a possibility; unkindness as lack of understanding, and so forth. With this in mind, the next time you are looking at a situation from a fixed point of view, do your best to pause, step back from "your view," and look at it from another angle; exercise your CI, take off the "blue lenses" that we spoke about earlier. The way that we interpret an event is exactly that: *our interpretation.* But it does not make it *the only* interpretation.

The Finer Distinctions

The finer distinctions are the more intricate details of our thoughts (typically referred to as *submodalities* (26) within the field of NLP). These details may include the colours, the clarity, the sounds and so forth.

It is these *finer distinctions* which can directly influence our emotions; however, the majority of us are completely oblivious of this connection. Therefore, we have little control over how our disempowering thoughts and memories (particularly) can tend to make us feel, as-and-when they may spring to mind. Nevertheless, before we observe how manipulating some of these finer distinctions can help to neutralise disempowering thoughts and memories (which may arise from negative subconscious programmes), let's first simply demonstrate their effectiveness on a positive memory.

For instance; can you recall when you were last at the beach (or some other pleasurable experience)? Once you remember this, picture that experience as *vividly* as possible. Can you feel the positive emotions associated with the memory?

Now, as you hold that picture of the beach within your mind's eye; notice the *finer distinctions* (details). For example; is the memory of the beach in black-and-white, or in colour? Is it really bright and near within your mind's eye, or is it rather dull and distant? Are you associated (in the first person) or dissociated (remembering the event through the eyes of a *third* party, thus seeing yourself in the picture)?

To further illustrate, let's go ahead and change some of these *distinctions*. In your mind's eye, if the memory is in colour, then change it into black and white. If the picture is really clear then make it fuzzy and blurry; if you picture the whole scene as really close to you, then make it further away. Now imagine the memory as if you were watching it on a black and white television.

Now that you have made these minor changes, does the memory still seem as interesting? Better still, does it have the same *emotional pull* that it had before? In your mind's eye, is that memory still as captivating and alluring as it was initially? In short; does it feel the same? Chances are that it doesn't.

So what's the point of this and how can it help? This can help because the same principle also applies with our undesirable memories. If you have a reoccurring memory (mental picture) of something that is bothering you, you could also rearrange a number of the *finer distinctions* with it.

For example; just as before, if the picture within your mind's eye is in colour, then change it into black and white. If it's close to you then make it far away. If you're looking through your own eyes in the memory then dissociate yourself and view the whole thing as if it were on television. If it is clear, then make it blurry, and so on.

If this has been done properly, it's very likely that once you have made a few of these changes to the *finer distinctions,* the negative memory will be far less compelling emotionally.

Consequently it will no longer have the same effect on you, thus it becomes easier to deal with—and is less of a barrier—if (and when) it arises. I once had a memory that would cause me to feel disempowered every single time that it sprung to mind, triggered by something or someone else. This literally went on for years, until I learnt of this simple technique.

Armed with this knowledge I then pictured that memory in my mind's eye, but I changed that picture into black-and-white instead of colour, and then I dissociated myself from it as if I were watching it on a black and white television. In my mind's eye, I then turned the volume all the way down on that television. Once I rearranged these simple details the memory itself became less vivid, and therefore less emotionally-gripping.

Whenever it arose I simply followed this procedure and nullified its "pulling power." And after a short while it *automatically* became less captivating without me having to consciously rearrange any of these finer distinctions. I had successfully changed the mechanism.

At this stage, you might be wondering whether this technique will be effective on *all* negative memories or thoughts. The answer is yes, potentially. But not necessarily by using the same format which has been described throughout this section.

The foregoing examples have simply been used to illustrate the effectiveness of this technique, and although the basic format listed can be highly effective for *mildly* unpleasant memories; those memories which are considered to be *traumatic,* in nature, may require a more advanced level of intervention.

__Finer Distinctions & Motivation__

There are some things that we are easily motivated toward; and
then there are things which we say we want to do, but somehow
we don't get around to doing them. The latter being
predominately due to *a lack of motivation*; so how do we
remedy this?

1) Firstly: within your mind's eye, picture something that
   you are naturally motivated to do and notice the *finer
   distinctions* within that picture. It's probably an alluring
   and captivating image of some sort. Perhaps you imagine
   it as a clear, bright and colourful picture which is close
   to you. You are probably also fully associated (looking
   through your own eyes, and hence cannot see yourself in
   the picture).

2) Now think of something that you want to do but haven't
   yet done, due to a lack of motivation. Chances are that
   this mental image is not represented as being close to
   you like the first one was (as it's at the "back of your
   mind"), neither will it be as clear, bright or colourful.
   Perhaps it's slightly dull and you are dissociated in the
   picture. In this case we now know what we can do to
   remedy this.

3) Change the *finer distinctions* of the non-motivated image
   (dull, distant, etc.) into the finer distinctions of the
   motivated image (bright, vivid, colourful, etc.) It should
   then automatically start to appear as more interesting and
   captivating, thus motivating you to *want* to move toward
   it.

This can also work, vice versa, for overcoming temptations. For instance, perhaps you are quitting chocolate, but regularly find yourself day dreaming about your favourite chocolate bar. Within your mind's eye, chances are that this picture is quite alluring and therefore stimulates the corresponding emotion.

So, just as we did earlier, if the picture is clear, colourful, bright, near and so on, reverse the *finer distinctions* and make it blurry, dull, far, small, and dissociated, within your mind's eye. By practicing this simple technique we can gain an advanced level of control over our thoughts and emotions. We cannot expect to control our lives if we do not exert the dominant level of control over our own thoughts.

Mind Food

The subconscious mind functions involuntarily, whether you make any effort to influence it or not, it will not remain idle. If you do not actively fill the subconscious mind with positive and uplifting information that it can manifest into your physical experiences: it will simply feed upon whatever other thoughts and stimuli that reach it, as a result of your neglect to take control of this process.

Just as your body needs food, as too does your mind. You can either feed it mental "junk food," or you can feed it some wholesome energizing and nutritious "food" that will help to keep it healthy and make you feel good in the process. Become more mindful of what you allow to influence you: *Mind Your Mind.* Imagine someone entered your home and started emptying their garbage on your carpet, you would have a problem with that right? Of course you would! Yet many of us willingly accept the garbage being dumped into the fabric of our minds on a daily basis: whether that be through the news (papers), propaganda, celebrity gossip, soap operas (many of which are based on adultery, lies and deceit) negative music, negative conversations, negative people, so on and so forth.

Uplifting Music – Motivational Books, DVDs & Audios

Once we have limited the intake of "mental junk food" we then need to fill that void with some positive and empowering influences. This could include regularly listening to some empowering audios or reading a page or two, each day, of a personal development book, *as you are doing right now*. If you do not have any of these within your current library at home, apart from this book, then there are many uplifting personal development books, audio programmes and DVDs on websites such as *YouTube*, *Amazon*, etc.

Following on from this, music also has a tremendous ability to influence our emotions. The effect that sounds and tones have on physical matter (and therefore the cells within your body) is made undeniably clear within the field of study known as *Cymatics*. Listening to some calming music, or at least music that does not promote negativity in any manner, will also promote a more positive perspective.

You may be surprised at how much love and abundance the world has to offer, and how much amazing opportunities are readily available to us every single day, once we attune ourselves to a more optimistic vibe (vibration) and consciously limit the intake of unnecessary negativity. As a result, many of the pessimistic thought patterns that form unnecessary boundaries—on how we view ourselves and the world—will dissipate, allowing new and empowering paradigms to emerge.

Ideas on Paper

Writing, like visualisation, is a psychoneuromuscular activity that can be used to deeply imprint information within the subconscious mind. Writing down our ideas and accomplishments etc., can also help to strengthen our focus, our organization skills, and simply serve as a powerful visual reminder. And the more that we repeatedly look at them, the deeper the imprint upon the subconscious mind and therefore the closer we become to manifesting those ideas and exceeding those accomplishments. To add to this; *writing down your ideas on paper can be the very first step of you bringing them into physical existence.*

Positive Thinking

As we now know, how you perceive the external world is a direct reflection of your internal world: *your state of consciousness.* An overall optimistic attitude toward our capabilities and our lives in general is essential. Whenever we find ourselves thinking thoughts of doubt and scarcity, we can now use some of the simple techniques that we have learnt to counteract the process.

Listen: *You have great power within you. You are a direct expression of the same source that creates all that you perceive and more. You have the sum-total of all the wisdom of your ancestors encoded within your DNA and you are intrinsically connected to the Infinitely Vast Creative Intelligence which permeates every aspect of existence. And now that your awareness has, once again, been brought to this unlimited resource you will consciously utilise it to a greater degree.*

In closing: *Although we are all kindred souls (interconnected energy); until we meet in person, I strongly believe that we have certainly met, through these pages. Let us now go forth into the world equipped with these insights so that we may contribute to the betterment of humanity by Achieving More, Becoming More, Utilising More and Perceiving More: thereby inspiring others to do the same.*

By transcending perceived limitations we are able to make the shift into the next stage of consciousness; utilising a higher degree of our true unlimited potential, collectively.

Remember, other than those of the mind, some of the greatest resources are those of the character, and your character is ultimately tailored in accordance with your most dominant thoughts. Should you decide to sincerely take heed of the principles found within this book, then the information herein has duly served its purpose as an inspirational catalyst.

On the other hand, now that you have been exposed to this information, should you decide *not* to call forth, and utilise, the phenomenal abundance of potential power within you, then remember...

"The Only One Stopping You, is You!"

The End of Part Four

The Beginning

"If you don't start somewhere, then you won't get anywhere."
– Bob Marley

TEST YOUR KNOWLEDGE

Here's a chance to test your knowledge with a book quiz. All of the questions are based on the information within this book and categorised by chapter.

The intent of the quiz is not only to challenge you on what you have discovered throughout this book, but also to help embed the information, within your mind, so that it has a longer lasting impact upon your personal development.

Research shows that when we have to remember something, i.e. while doing a quiz, once remembered it becomes less likely to be forgotten again.

This will help you to make the most of what you have learnt throughout the course of this book, and also increase your ability to effectively remember the information when in need.

Have fun.

CORNERSTONE ONE

THE PRESENT OF PRESENCE

The more we point the finger at others, what are we communicating to ourselves?

Life will keep presenting us with persons, places and things that are...?

Being more present simply means...?

What is a simple way to bring your attention into the present moment?

Why is the present moment all that ever truly exists?

What controls your destiny; your past, or the decisions that you are making right now?

GOAL SCORING

By challenging spectators on their opinions, engaging in unnecessary debates or arguments, we are wasting valuable...?

What is the difference between goal scoring and goal setting?

The major benefit of having goals is that they help to keep us...?

When advancing toward a goal that has been set, what is the one simple question that we must ask ourselves in the face of a new opportunity?

Why is it important to be specific with the goals that we set?

Strategy is the bridge between…?

What are the four questions we can ask to gain maximum clarity of a goal?

STEADFAST

Every desire starts with a…?

Many of us are so busy anticipating the big results that we habitually…?

An idea is the root seed of…?

What do many of us forget to consider when recognising the great achievements of others?

When our inner-drive is low, what is born?

What is the difference between steadfastness and inner-drive?

How can language affect our inner-drive?

List 5 ways that we can overcome any doubt and inertia?

PASSION

What is the importance of passion?

When is passion detrimental?

Why is passion a key component to achieving success in any endeavour?

Which is more compelling, an emotional driving force or a logical one?

What is the purpose of the passion board?

What is one of the greatest inhibitors to pursuing your passion?

The fear of failure is closely associated with…?

Which central fear is the source of all comparatives?

What is the importance of finding your *WHY*?

CORNERSTONE TWO

SELF WORTH

Life is not solely about having more, life is also about…?

The highest form of Self-Worth is…?

What are some of the attributes of someone that has a healthy level of self-worth?

What are some of the attributes of someone who has low self-worth?

What are some of the attributes of someone that is "unhealthily narcissistic?"

An overt character trait usually…?

Identifying our character strengths and weaknesses can lead to…?

Real and lasting self-worth is derived from…

When do you feel most void of self-worth?

What is the importance of self inventory?

What is the importance of a "positive morning ritual?"

List 7 ways to improve your level of self-worth.

CONFIDENCE

What is the difference between confidence and self worth?

What is the importance of multiple small achievements, when aiming to build lasting self confidence?

What is Anchoring and how is it useful?

Why is the "Swish Pattern" such a powerful means of replacing negative thought patterns?

What are 9 simple lifestyle adjustments that can enhance self-confidence, and why?

WHAT IS FEAR?

What are the differences between type 1 and type 2 fears?

The word "fear" is commonly used as a label for the release of…?

Why is the *word* itself fear, a weakness?

According to a study conducted in 2008, what percentage of our fears, actually happen to us? And what percentages of those are based on lack of knowledge?

Why is type 2 fear the most troublesome?

What are some of the side effects of constant unsubstantiated fear?

What are some of the short term benefits of adrenaline?

The label that we give something is what determines what that thing…?

BALANCE

What are some of the similarities between humans and the planet?

What are the three major areas and what is the importance of growth within all three of them?

Name some of the simple ways to implement more variety into a routine?

What is the relationship between balance and burnout?

What is usually the main cause of a "mental block?

Name some ways that we can overcome a mental block?

List 3 benefits of being within the Hakalau?

What is another name for the Hakalau?

What is the "pendulum swing effect" and why is controlling it important for long term change?

CORNERSTONE THREE

SELF AWARENESS

Give some examples of "surface attributes?"

What is the difference between the "cause" and the "effect?"

Where does the word personality originate from?

Various elements of the personality are also shaped by…?

What is emotional intelligence?

What is the importance of congruence in self-awareness?

What is the difference between self-consciousness and self-awareness?

How does frustration validate the ego?

What is the purpose of the question; "what am I thinking right now?"

BELIEF SYSTEMS

Beliefs gain power with…?

What are shortcut beliefs and how do we use them?

What are limiting beliefs and how do they affect us?

What are core beliefs and how do they affect us?

"Any limiting belief concerning one's ability can be uprooted and replaced fairly easily. And one of the most effective ways to achieve this is simply to…?"

List 6 of the most common limiting beliefs

Why is the belief that "failure is bad," one of the most limiting beliefs of all?

The belief that "failure is bad" is almost inseparable from the belief that…?

How can excuses become limiting beliefs?

In reality, all events that happen in life are completely…?

List some examples of empowering beliefs.

CORNERSTONE FOUR

THE MAP

What is "The Map?"

What is our view of reality biased by?

What is Deletion?

What is Distortion?

What is Generalisation?

When we delete, distort or generalise information this is based on…?

How does becoming more aware of when we are deleting, distorting or generalising information contribute to perceiving more?

What determines how we feel is never the experience itself, but rather…?

MIND YOUR MIND

What is "Universal Mind?"

Do we use more than 10 percent of our brain?

Explain the difference between using 10 percent of the brain's mass and 10 percent of the brain's potential.

Within Western based brain research, why was it originally thought that we only use 10 percent of the brain's mass?

What are the known functions of the Gilal Cells?

What is the Subconscious Mind, and what are its main faculties?

How does the subconscious mind relate to the brain?

How does the subconscious relate to involuntary actions?

How does the subconscious relate to memory?

How does the subconscious relate to skill?

What is the Conscious Mind, and what are its main faculties?

Why is the conscious mind considered to be "the sentinel?"

What is the relationship between the conscious and the subconscious mind?

Why are many subconscious patterns picked up before the age of ten?

What, and where, is super-consciousness?

What is Context-Intelligence and why is it important?

What is the relationship between the conscious mind, the subconscious mind and super-consciousness?

What is the relationship between the human brain and super-consciousness?

Why is the "empty" space between you and this book, far from empty?

What are the benefits behind the use of affirmations?

What is meant by "emotionalised thought" and what is the importance of this in relation to affirmations?

How does the language that we use affect us, for better or worse?

What is Reframing and how can it help?

What are The Finer Distinctions and how can they help?

Name some ways in which we can create positive influences to feed our mind.

GENERAL QUESTIONS

If you could condense all of the information you have learnt throughout this book into one key message, what would that message be?

What chapter within this book was the most gripping for you, and why?

What have you achieved as a result of reading this book?

How has this book contributed toward you becoming a better person?

AFFIRMATION

(Note: please see section on affirmations within the chapter: *Mind Your Mind* - page 297 - before using the affirmations listed here). Here is a complete affirmation that you can use at least once every day:

I am an expression of the same source that creates worlds, galaxies and universes

I am nature, nature is me

I am creation, creation is me

I am love, love is me

I am the universe, the universe is me

I am true to me

I am honest with me

I am loyal to me

I like me, I like *being* me

I love me, I love *being* me

I am *beyond* confident in me

I have unwavering belief in me

I completely trust me

I am aware *of* me

I am aware *in* me

I *am* me

I AM

ONE LINER AFFIRMATIONS

1. I make the most of the present moment
2. I feel more aware now, than ever before
3. I am aware, I notice opportunities as and when they arise
4. I can achieve anything that I put my mind to
5. I can see my goal, therefore I can reach it
6. I'm an effective goal scorer
7. I am able to steadfast
8. I have persistence
9. I have inner drive
10. I am passionate about…
11. I have strong self confidence, strong self worth and strong self esteem.
12. I love me
13. I am strong, I push beyond imaginary fears
14. Every day I become even more aware of my abilities
15. I improve at least 1% every single day
16. My positive beliefs are strong, my negative beliefs are weak
17. Day by day my perception is enhancing.
18. Through the power of my mind, I am creator of my life's circumstances.
19. I am truly grateful for the power of the mind
20. My mind is one with Universal Mind
21. My mind is infinite

22. I am infinitely grateful for…

BIBLIOGRAPHY

1. **Serafin, Tatiana.** Rags to Riches Billionaires. *Forbes.com.* [Online] 2006. http://www.forbes.com/2007/06/22/billionaires-gates-winfrey-biz-cz_ts_0626rags2riches.html.

2. **Daily, Smart Money.** Ten Rags to Riches Billionaires. *smartmoneydaily.com.* [Online] http://www.smartmoneydaily.com/celeb-finance/10-rags-to-riches-billionaires.aspx.

3. **Tolle, Eckhart.** *A New Earth.* New York : Plume (A member of the Penguin Group), 2006, p. 139.

4. **Jackson, Robert Greene and Curtis.** Chapter 1: See things for what they are - intense realism. *The 50th Law.* New York : Harper Studios, an imprint of Harper Collins Publishers, 2009.

5. **Alofsin, Anthony.** *Frank Lloyd Wright - The Lost Years, 1910-1922: A Study of Influence.* Chicago and London, UK : University of Chicago Press, 1993, p. 359.

6. **Pythalos, Justin.** My Morning Ritual: How to be Productive, Happy and Healthy Everyday. *YouTube.* [Online] 7 March 2012. http://www.youtube.com/watch?v=PliFBr__T7Y.

7. **Robbins, Tony.** Tony Robbins on Rituals. *YouTube.* [Online] 15 June 2009. http://www.youtube.com/watch?v=9VHdquVp7wM.

8. **About.com.** Top Ten Reasons to Smile. *About.com.* [Online] 4 February 2010. http://longevity.about.com/od/lifelongbeauty/tp/smiling.htm.

9. Anchoring. *nlpworld.co.uk.* [Online]
http://www.nlpworld.co.uk/nlp-glossary/a/anchoring/.

10. **Pavlov, Ivan P.** Pavlov's Dogs - Conditioned Reflexes.
books.google.co.uk. [Online]
http://books.google.co.uk/books?hl=en&lr=&id=cknrYDqAClkC&oi=fn
d&pg=PR9&dq=Pavlov%E2%80%99s+Dogs+%E2%80%93+Conditione
d+Reflex&ots=Kzspi8Y6Fa&sig=ej70-
l8wKyIzNZBkSac3AonbEnY#v=onepage&q=Pavlov%E2%80%99s%20D
ogs%20%E2%80%93%20Conditioned%20Reflex&f=false.

11. Classical Conditionong. *wikipedia.org.* [Online]
http://en.wikipedia.org/wiki/Classical_conditioning.

12. **Gong, QI.** The Creative Power of Visualisation.
myqigong.wordpress.com. [Online]
http://myqigong.wordpress.com/tag/russian-olympic-athletes/.

13. **Institute, The Franklin.** Resources for Science Learning - Imagine
Increased Mustle Strength! Experiment. *www.fi.edu.* [Online]
http://www.fi.edu/learn/brain/exercise.html.

14. **Vladimir M. Zatsiorsky and William J. Kraemer, PhD.** *Science and
Practice of Strength Training.* s.l. : The Library of Congress, 2006.

15. **Wattles, Wallace D.** *The Science of Getting Rich.* s.l. : Filiquarian
Publishing, p. 8.

16. Public Self Consciousness. *wikipedia.org.* [Online]
http://en.wikipedia.org/wiki/Self-consciousness.

17. The Charisma Mystery. *YouTube.* [Online] BostonMOS, 6
December 2012. http://youtube.com/watch?v=pQQ9lPOqlrw.

18. **Robbins, Tony.** *Awaken the Giant Within.* 1 November 1992.

19. **Cialdini, Dr. Robert.** *Influence! The Psychology of Persuasion.* New York : Harper Collins Publishers, 2007, p. 5.

20. **Radwan, Farouk.** How Beliefs are Formed. *2knowmyself.com.* [Online] http://www.2knowmyself.com/How_beliefs_are_formed.

21. **Forer, Bertram R.** The Forer Effect. *Wikipedia.com.* [Online] http://en.wikipedia.org/wiki/Forer_effect.

22. **Beyerstein, Barry L.** *Mind Myths: Exploring Popular Assumptions About the Mind and Brain.* Chichester, Sussex, UK : John Wiley & Sons, 1999, pp. 3-24.

23. **Hill, Napoleon.** *Think and Grow Rich.* West Sussex, UK : Capstone Publishing, 2009, pp. 305-306.

24. **Library, Mind Reach.** Our Three Brains. *cosmic-mindreach.com.* [Online] http://www.cosmic-mindreach.com/Three-Brains.html.

25. **Jeffers, Susan.** *Feel the Fear and do it Anyway - Pain to Power Vocabulary.* Reading, UK : Vermillion (an imprint of Ebury Publishing, a Random House Group Company), 2007, p. 37.

26. The Finer Distinctions: Submodalities. *nlpworld.co.uk.* [Online] http://www.nlpworld.co.uk/nlp-glossary/s/submodalities/.

SPEAKING

Having spoken for a number of organizations throughout the UK, Matt Matthews is able to convey his message with clarity, simplicity and charisma. Matt has the versatility to engage various age groups with either one of his keynote speeches, the first of which is:

Goal Scoring
Goal Scoring is a speech that focuses on the importance of following through to achieve goals that have been set. Matt often says that it's one thing to set goals, but another thing to follow through with fierce determination toward their accomplishment. If you are looking for a keynote speech which will empower an audience and inspire them to *overcome adversity with focused drive and determination*, then look no further. Prepared to be truly inspired by ***Goal Scoring!***

Doubt Your Doubts & Limit Your Limits
In this keynote, Matt highlights the most common doubts that prevent many of us from taking action. This is a passionate and insightful high powered speech, guaranteed to inspire an audience to breakthrough limitation and manifest their excellence. This speech is particularly suited toward college and university students.

In addition to these keynote speeches Matt's most commonly requested topics are: Youth Enrichment, Overcoming Adversity, and Peak Performance Strategies. Matt is also available to speak on any of the topics found throughout this book.

If you are seeking a compelling inspirational speaker or peak performance strategist for your next event, please call 0203 292 1391 or simply complete and return the form on the next page.

Matt Matthews Enterprises
88 – 90 Hatton Garden
London
EC1N 8PN
www.mattmatthews.co

I am interested in learning more about Matt Matthews Enterprises.
Please send me the FREE goal scoring spreadsheet.

My name is_____

Address_____

City/County/Post Code_____

Telephone #: (Home) _____ (Bus.) _____

Email _____

I would like more information about:

a.____ *"The Only One Stopping You, is You!"* Workshops

b.____ Upcoming Events

c.____ Booking Matt as a Speaker

d.____ Booking Matt as a Coach

I would like to order _____ copies of this book

@ £8.00 (per unit) bulk price (over 20 copies) or £12.99 individually.

Postage and Packaging: add £1.50 per book for single orders.

£15.00 - £40.00 for bulk orders of 20 - 100 copies

£40.00 - £130.00 for bulk orders of 101 – 500 copies.

Total Amount Enclosed (ck/mo) _____

Please make all cheques payable to Matt Matthews Enterprises

Make a copy of this page, fill it out, and then send it to the above address.
Alternatively fax a copy to 0203 292 1391 or scan/email to: admin@mattmatthews.co

Lightning Source UK Ltd.
Milton Keynes UK
UKOW06f0002170316

270291UK00016B/234/P